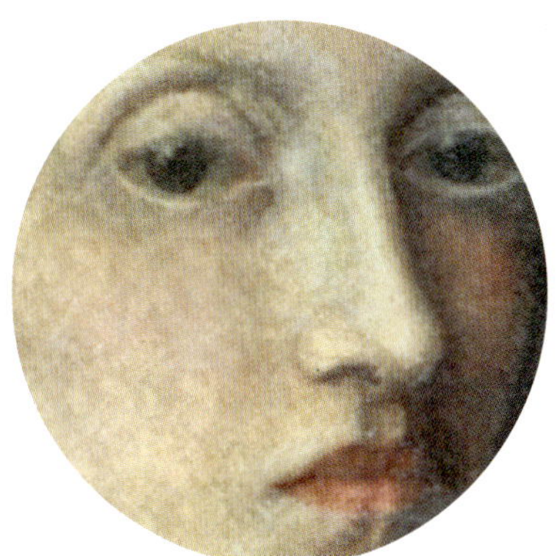

Now I see you dying
Now I see you flying
faces through the mist

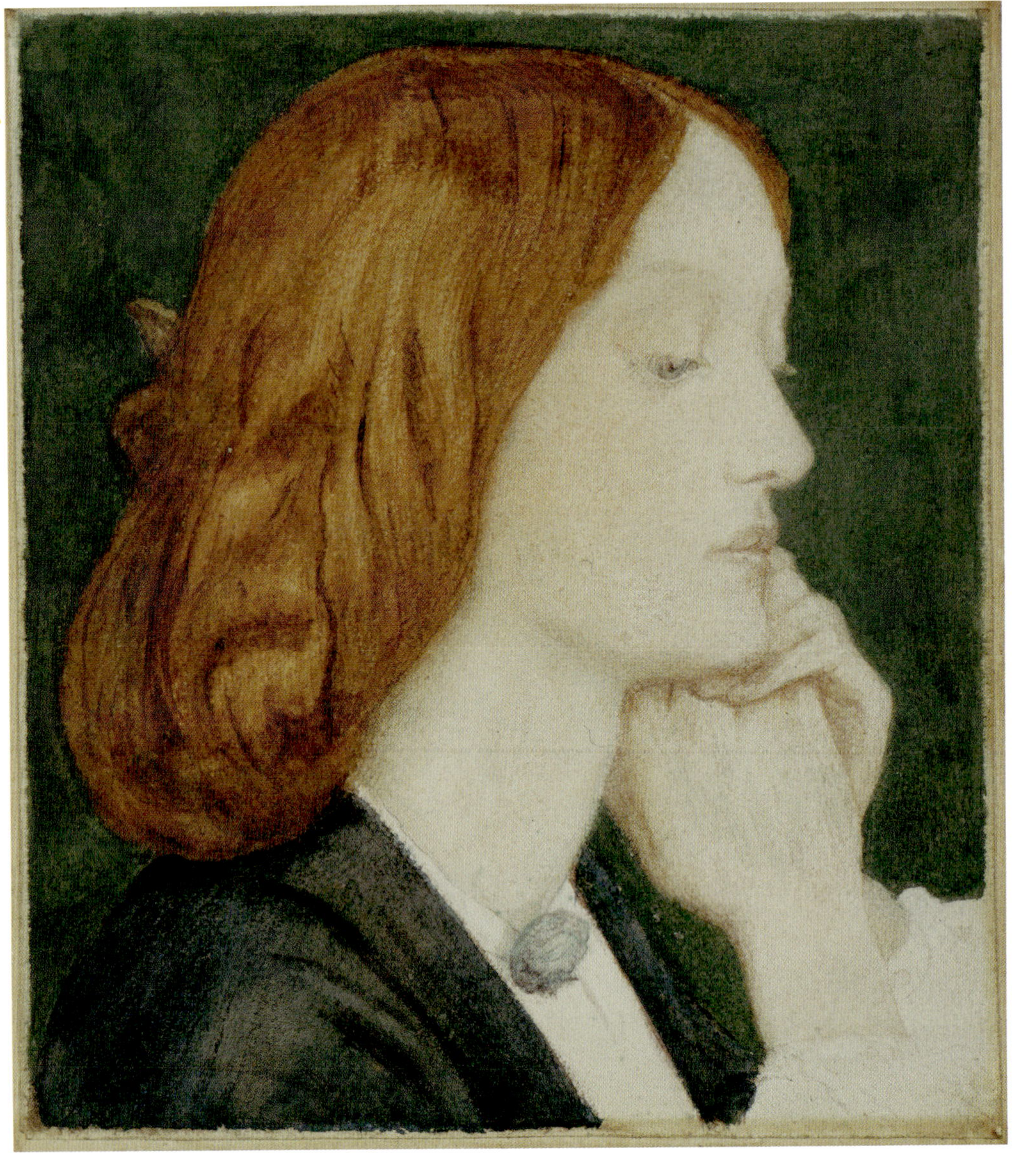

ELIZABETH SIDDAL

Her Story

Jan Marsh

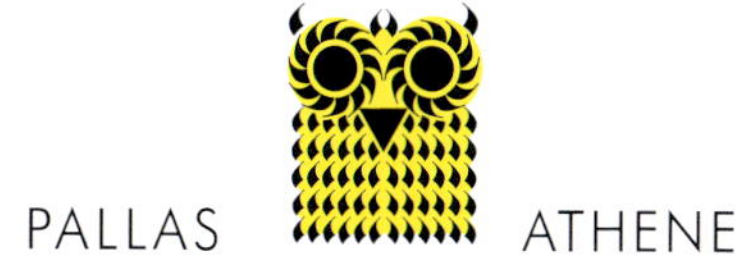

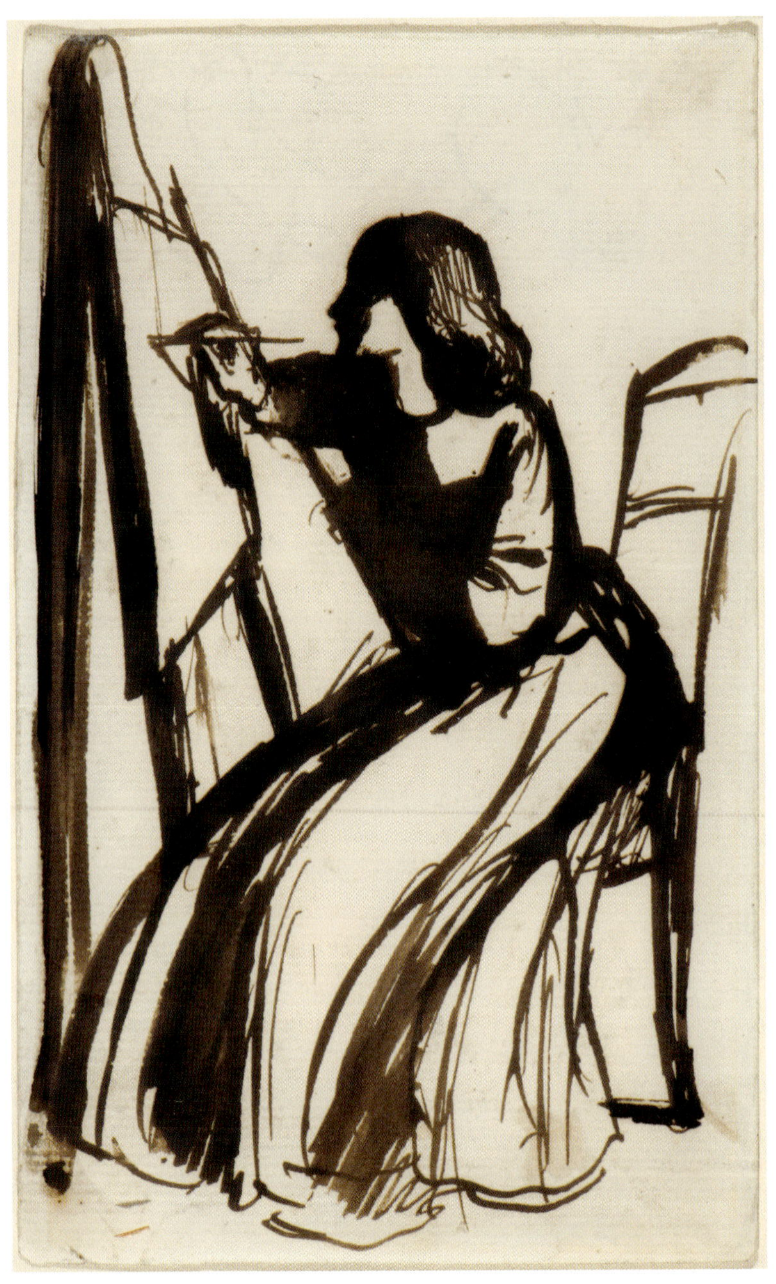

CONTENTS

Opposite: D. G. Rossetti, Sketch of Elizabeth Siddal at the Easel, (approximately actual size), c. 1852

Frontispiece (p. 2): D. G. Rossetti, Portrait of Elizabeth Siddal, 1854

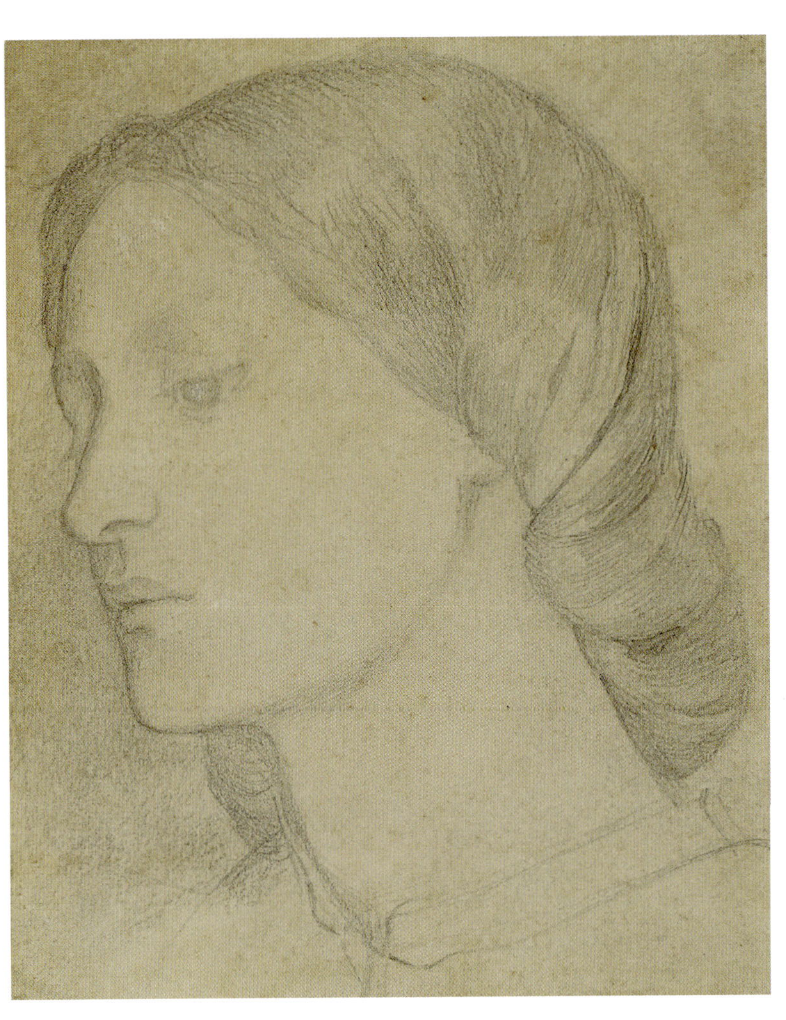

In biography you have your little handful of facts, little bits of a puzzle, and you sit and think, and fit 'em together this way and that, and get up and throw 'em down and say damn, and go out for a walk.

Robert Louis Stevenson, 18 June 1893

PREFACE

The first, and indeed only, obituary of Elizabeth Siddal was published in the *Sheffield and Rotherham Independent* on 18 February 1862.[1] Written by William Ibbitt, artist and silversmith, who knew Siddal during her visit to the city in 1857, it was based on her own account of her life. This made no mention of modelling for the painters of the Pre-Raphaelite Brotherhood, but told the story of a dressmaker with ambitions to become an artist, who had secured the patronage of John Ruskin, and exhibited with the PRB.

Over 20 years later, when Pre-Raphaelite histories began to appear, Siddal was cited only as the beautiful model and muse, romantically discovered working in a bonnet shop, who had become the sickly, tragic wife of Dante Gabriel Rossetti. In the first biographical account of Siddal, published in 1903, Rossetti's brother William listed 24 artworks and reconstructed 13 poems from drafts. But clearly ignorant of the Sheffield obituary, he concluded that, despite the feebleness of both pictures and verses, she was 'a woman of unusual capacities, worthy of being espoused to a painter and poet'.[2]

Thereafter, more or less imaginative iterations of Siddal's life story cast her as a dove, a betrayed beloved, a doomed victim, a drug addict, a supermodel and a Pre-Raphaelite icon. The present book ascertains what can be factually known and inferred about Elizabeth Siddal's life from contemporary sources. Sadly, it can't aspire to the account she herself would have written, but it does aim to dispose of myths and misinterpretations.

Opposite: D. G. Rossetti, Portrait head of Elizabeth Siddal (approximately actual size), date unknown

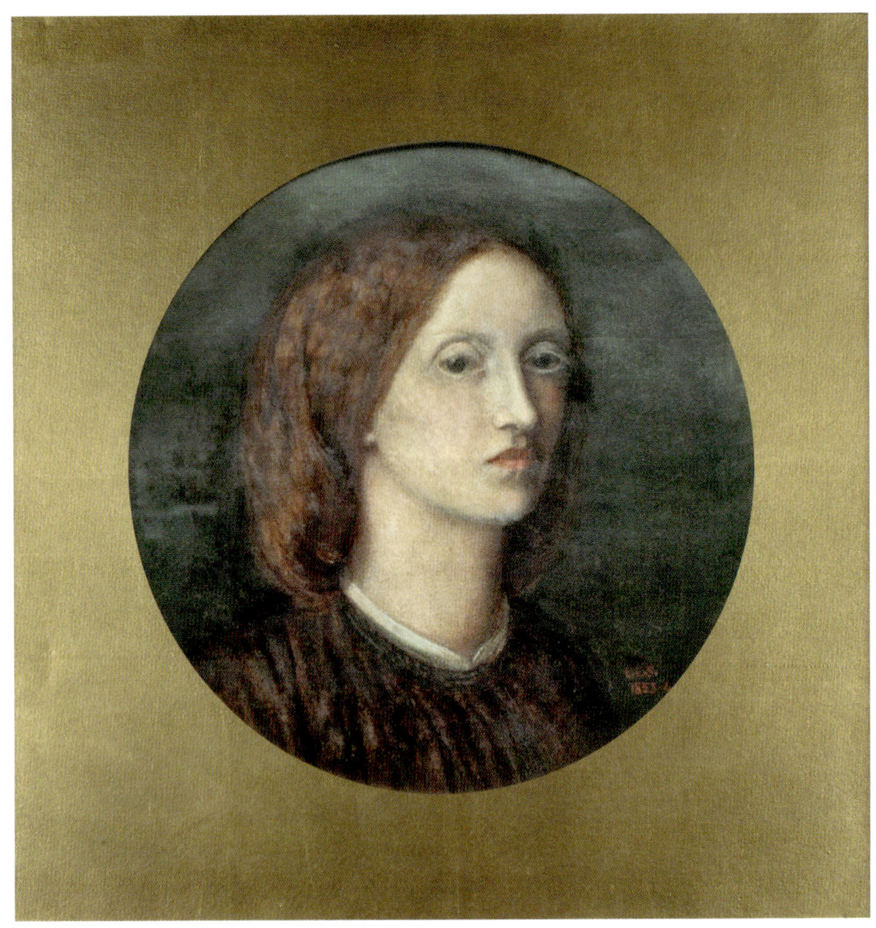

E. E. Siddal, Self-Portrait, 1853-4

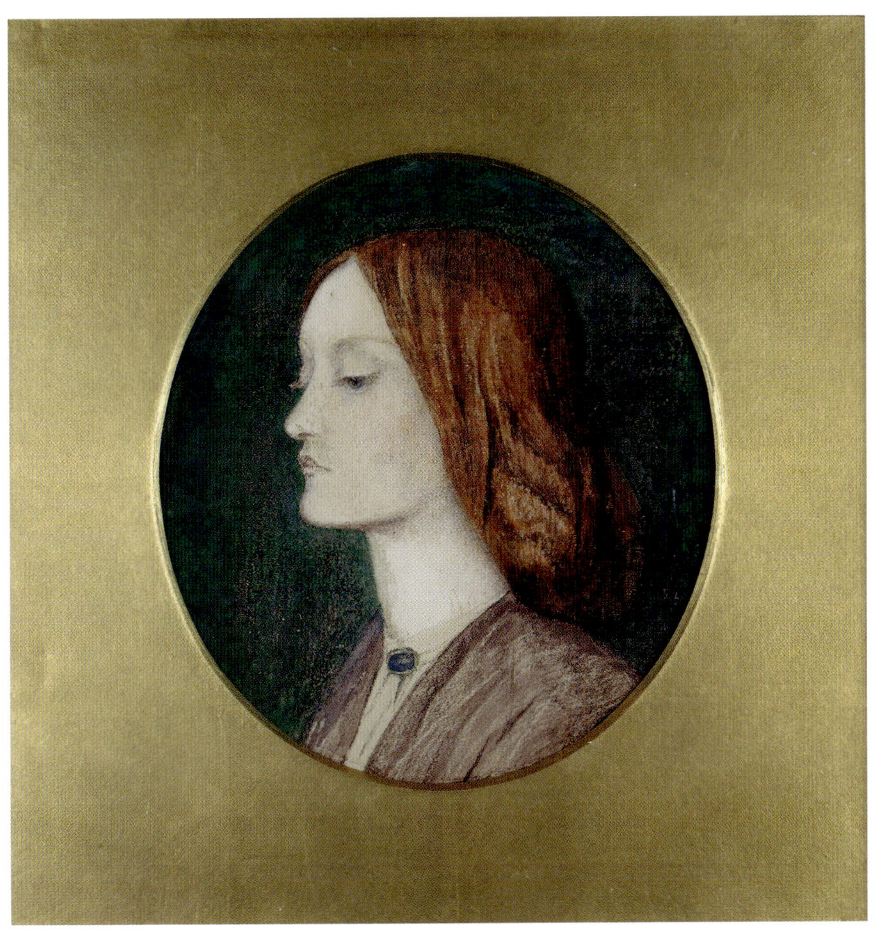

D. G. Rossetti, Portrait of Elizabeth Siddal, 1854

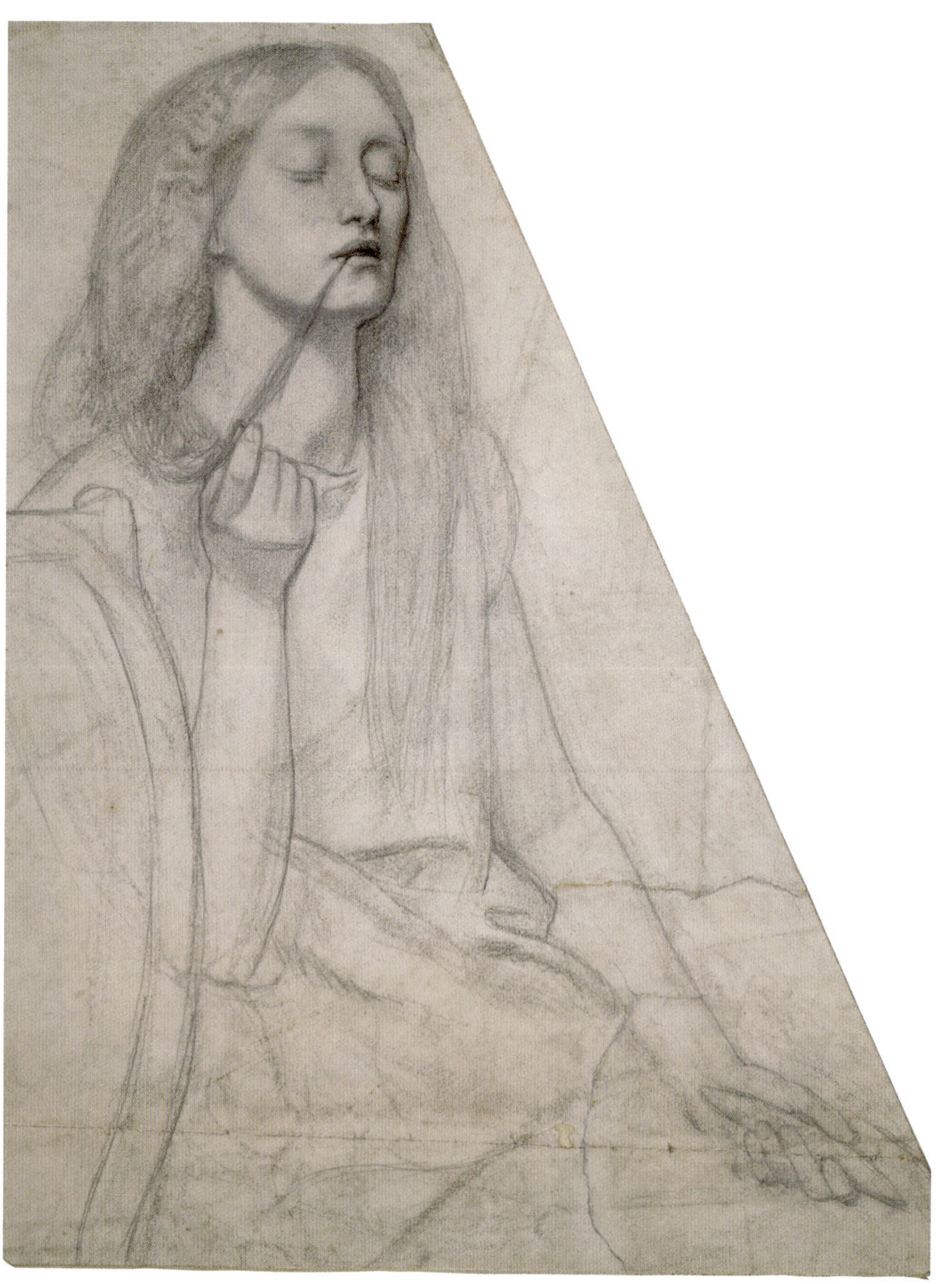

1.
MODEL

Opposite: *D. G. Rossetti, Study for Delia, 1853. Illustration to a Latin poem in which the poet's beloved dreamily imagines his return*

LET'S BEGIN AT THE BEGINNING, to trace out what is known of Elizabeth Siddal's life as best we can. The sources are fragmentary but, like a jigsaw puzzle with missing pieces, when assembled may yield a narrative picture.

We can start with her birth, in July 1829 in the Holborn area of London, one of eight children born to Elizabeth Eleanor, formerly Evans, wife of Charles Siddall, maker and retailer of cutlery and bladed tools. He was from Sheffield, centre of skilled craftsmen producing sharp 'edge tools': knives, scissors, razors, chisels. The family moved to different homes and by 1849 were living on the Old Kent Road in Southwark, with a shop on the street and rooms above. The district was a thriving mix of lower-middle and working-class households. One childhood memory recounted by Elizabeth was of a neighbour who lifted her over the muddy roadway—and was later hanged for murdering his lover.

Maybe that grew in the retelling, although the dates fit, and the remembrance fits with her liking for melodramatic and macabre tales.

In Victorian terms, Charles Siddall was 'in trade' and therefore not a 'gentleman'. But the family was not impoverished. There were tales of the Siddalls, in the Derbyshire village of Hope, having once been gentry, with armorial bearings. The sons Charles, James and Henry were trained to carry on the cutlery business; the daughters' occupation was entered in the national census as 'dressmaker', meaning they too worked from home, making and remaking women's garments as fashions evolved. The census lists no live-in servants, but it is likely that daily cleaners and washerwomen were employed. Mrs Siddall's sister Lucy and her husband William Day kept a grocery shop in Islington, an area of middle-class villas. When in 1855 Gabriel Rossetti visited the Siddall home in Southwark, he was relieved to report that his sweetheart's 'native crib' was 'comfortable'.[1] Her family was not working class and later acquaintances noted that she spoke without grammatical errors or a local accent.

She had discovered the poetry of Tennyson by reading some verses in paper used to wrap groceries.[2] Like most girls of her era, she will have been mainly homeschooled in literacy, numeracy, scripture, sewing, and perhaps 'ladylike' manners. No more personal details of Elizabeth's youth are known. According to William Rossetti, two sisters—Clara and Lydia—and two brothers—James and Harry—were still around in 1900,[3] but no-one sought them to ask about their sister's early life.

Her first 'appearance' in the art world was in the last weeks of 1849, when she posed for the artist Walter Deverell. She was dressed in costume as the character of Viola in Shakespeare's *Twelfth Night*, in disguise as the boy Cesario.

Ignore for the moment the familiar but uncorroborated tale of Walter discovering Lizzie working in a milliner's shop. It dates from the 1880s when all the witnesses were dead. In 1857, Lizzie gave a different account to friends in Sheffield. In this, she said she had become acquainted with the Deverell family as a dressmaker, and had then 'shown some outlines, designs of her own leisure hours'[4] to Walter's father, who was principal of the government-funded School of Design in London. Through his encouragement, she met Walter and members of the Pre-Raphaelite Brotherhood, including Rossetti and Holman Hunt.

This narrative is itself untrustworthy—the details given or retained were doubtless incomplete—but it includes the vital detail of Lizzie's artistic endeavours (her own drawings) before she met the PRBs; these aspirations shaped later events. It glides over another detail, which is her initiative in approaching Mr Deverell, presumably to ask his opinion—a rather bold step for a young woman, but explicable if she was applying to enrol in

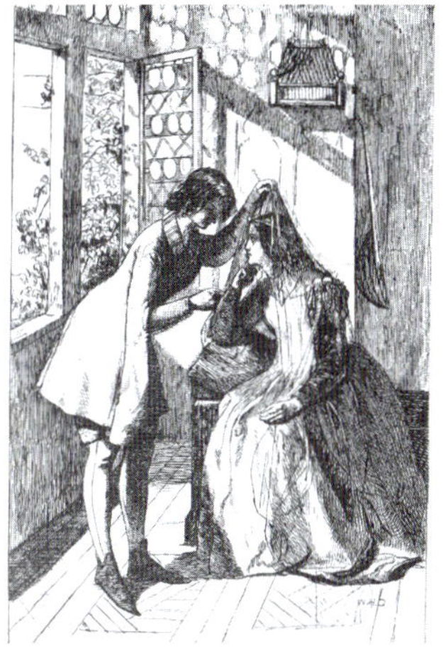

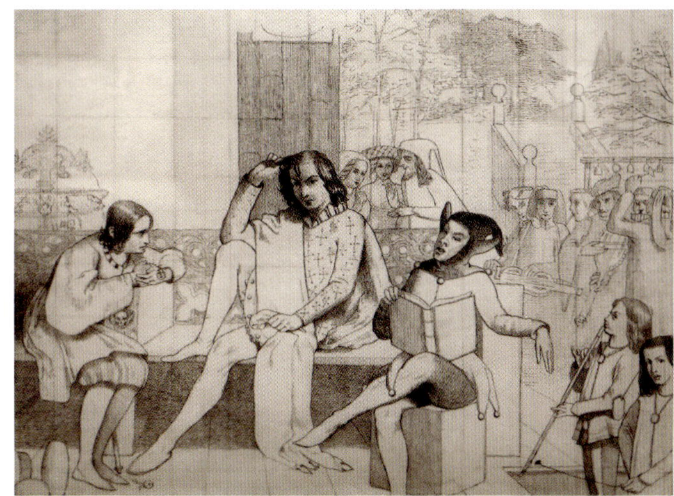

Left: Etching by W. H. Deverell, Viola and Olivia from Twelfth Night, published in The Germ, 1850

Right: W. H. Deverell, Study for 'If Music be the Food of Love', from Twelfth Night, 1849–50. From left to right: Siddal as Viola, Deverell as Orsino, Rossetti as Feste

a daytime class at the School of Design. One can't immediately imagine what her 'own designs' depicted. Perhaps they illustrated literary or biblical texts, like some of her later works. Maybe they were fashion sketches like those printed in the new weekly magazines. My best guess is that they were imaginative images, prompted by poetic sources, in the manner of the illustrated anthologies that surged into popularity in the late 1840s, with elaborate steel engravings and decorative devices. One possibility is that they were inspired by Tennyson's popular poems like 'The Lady of Shalott', which was the subject of her first Pre-Raphaelite drawing.

One likely response from Mr Deverell would have been encouragement to study in the School's female classes. Aimed at those needing to earn, these classes in draughtsmanship and basic design were appropriate to those working in the fashion trades, or to women employed colouring up engraved prints.

It is not known that Siddal took any such class. She seems

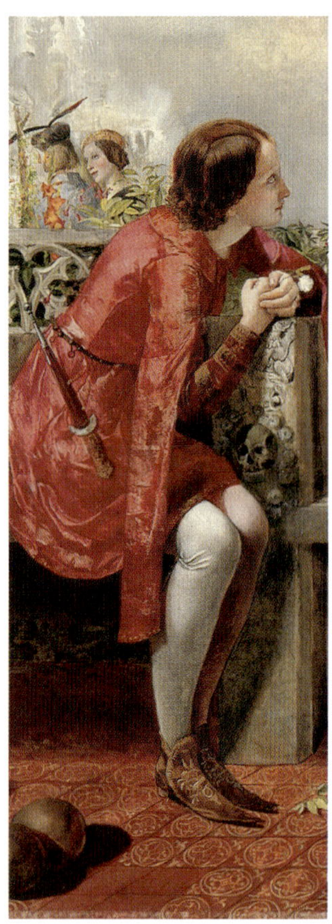

W. H. Deverell, detail from Scene from Twelfth Night (1849–50)

to have had higher aspirations towards fine art, and possibly saw more potential in the studios, agreeing or even offering to pose for Walter. He had been over-ambitious in creating a multi-figure scene from *Twelfth Night*, destined for the next summer exhibition at the Royal Academy. The modelling sessions took place in December 1849, either in the School of Design, where Walter taught alongside his father, or in the Deverell home. Lizzie took at least two poses—one profile pose listening as Count Orsino laments his love for the Lady Olivia, and one raising Olivia's veil, as Cesario woos as Orsino's messenger. The first was painted on to the large canvas, the second transformed into an etching for the PRB magazine *The Germ*. The first gives an accurate rendering of Siddal's pale, translucent skin and bright auburn hair (pictorially cut short); the second, in the words of William Rossetti 'does not give much idea, but is not unlike her in a way…'

What's remarkable is that in both images Cesario wears male attire, dressed as a page boy with tunic over tights, in garments borrowed—perhaps literally—from a stage-costume box. Such boyish outfits were worn by young ingénue performers with shapely legs to please theatre audiences. Offstage, women always wore long skirts. Siddal's willingness to pose wearing tights seems eloquent of her liking for studio life. She evidently then agreed or volunteered to pose for Deverell's friends.

Over the winter of 1849–50, as Holman Hunt was painting a crowded scene of a native British family rescuing a Christian priest from Druid attack, he had 'bothers with models', according to William Rossetti's record of PRB activities. With Lizzie's availability, the figure of an old woman was changed to that of a girl, clad in hessian, tending to the wounded priest. Later, Hunt asserted that because the figure was conceived as having the 'rough character' of an ancient Briton, his image did not convey

Siddal's 'grace or refinement'. She looks recognisable, however. Siddal was evidently a useful rather than a glamorous model.

If she went to see her likenesses at the summer exhibitions,[5] she may have been with her father or mother. It was customary for young women to be accompanied in public. More likely she went with Deverell. At the RA she will have seen Millais's *Christ in the House of his Parents,* which provoked a hostile howl from Charles Dickens for its ugly depiction of the Holy Family.

Lizzie told her Sheffield friend Mr Ibbitt that Walter had proposed marriage. Not implausible: he was good-looking and high-spirited, sharing Lizzie's taste for the theatre as well as art and literature. At 20, she was the age to seek a husband. But it is improbable, because Walter, aged 23, was not in a position to propose. He had yet to succeed as a painter, he was deputising for his father at the School of Design, and his health was poor. Lizzie's hope of a partnership was surely wishful thinking.

Hardly any direct testimony in diaries or letters by Elizabeth Siddal survives, so all previous accounts of Siddal's life—including my own—draw on the words of contemporaries and later commentators. They are not misleading, but naturally convey their authors' perspectives. Life writers therefore deploy creative imagination akin to fictional narrative as an alternative route into biography, ideally allied to historical rigour that keeps strictly to known facts. My aim here is to chronicle known events as they unfolded, with as little hindsight as possible.

Modelling, especially in the studios of unmarried young men, was not a respectable practice. Siddal's willingness to pose bespeaks disrespect for convention as well as a liking for art. No recollections mention a chaperone. In August 1850 she was again in Hunt's studio, modelling for his next painting, a scene from *Two Gentlemen of Verona*. This was a challenging pose, kneeling as Sylvia while Valentine intervenes to prevent Proteus's sexual

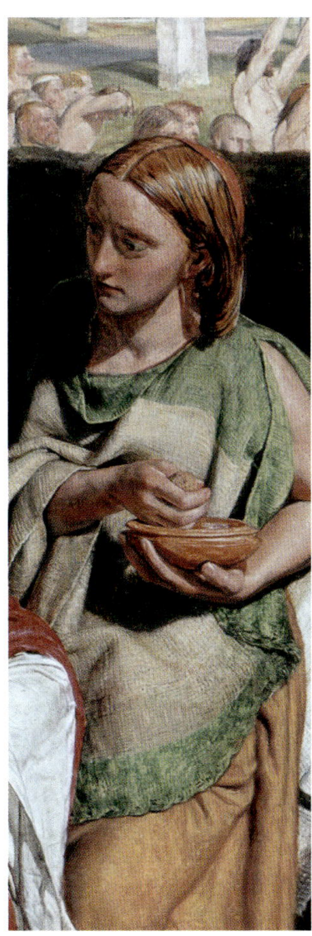

W. Holman Hunt, detail from British Family Sheltering a Christian Priest, 1850. Siddal modelled an 'ancient Briton' rescuing a priest from Druids in the Roman era

assault. The studio in Prospect Place on the river at Chelsea was also the location for some high-spirits—in Gabriel Rossetti's words, 'a disgraceful hoax'—when Hunt, their close friend and fellow PRB Fred Stephens, and Lizzie led two visitors to believe that she and Hunt were married. The victims of this jest were Jack Tupper and his father, whose firm had printed *The Germ*. Rossetti was dismayed, urging Hunt to apologise to the Tuppers. Lizzie evidently joined in the joke; no apology was due to her. She must have enjoyed the fun. Later, she would lament that the PRBs paid no heed to her 'soul'—her artistic and moral aims—but she may never have told Hunt of her desire to paint.

How did she explain herself at home? Later, she was noted for her reserve and disdain, so though it's hard to think of what explanation would cover daytime visits to Chelsea, it's possible she said nothing about modelling. It is unlikely that the Siddalls approved, but in July 1850 she was legally independent at the age of 21.

Later, William Rossetti stated that Lizzie ignored social conventions, 'was very little in the way of polite visiting' and preferred to do as she pleased. She returned to Hunt's studio early in 1851, as he resumed work on *Two Gentlemen*, the woodland background having being painted out of doors in the autumn. Not too many sessions would be needed to complete the figure of Sylvia. The painting was duly submitted to the Royal Academy in April. Writing to *The Times*, the critic John Ruskin, who now positioned himself as defender of the PRB, undercut his support for the new naturalism by noting the 'commonness of feature' in the face of Sylvia, in his view, owing to 'the unfortunate type chosen' as model.[6] Lizzie apparently looked too unrefined for a fictional duke's daughter. Hunt repainted the head with a more idealised aspect. Siddal was not in demand for her beauty. According to Arthur Hughes, a close friend of the PRBs, Siddal was 'tall and slender, with red, coppery hair and bright consumptive complexion, though in these early years she had no striking signs of ill health'.[7]

Hunt spent the autumn of 1851 with Millais and Charles Collins in Surrey, painting a moonlight background for his next work, showing Christ holding a lantern. The composition was sketched in his studio. Originality of subject was jealously guarded by artists and Siddal's involvement with Hunt's art led to a special journey to Chelsea with information about a similar composition she saw in a religious bookshop. If she hoped close acquaintance with the young painters would advance her own efforts, there is no evidence that this happened. In November she went to pose for Gabriel Rossetti, then working in Madox Brown's studio; here she wore a shift and held a long strand of loose hair to her lips, as the figure of Delia dreams of her lover's return. This was her first significant meeting with Rossetti, as he later recorded in an elaborate ink drawing inscribed '1851–1860', (see p. 110) but it did not result in any immediate romance. Instead, she agreed to model in the new year as Ophelia for Millais, who had completed a luxuriant riverbank background for the scene. She was also 'booked' by Collins, preparing a picture of St Elizabeth of Hungary.

Although there are no references to it, this sequence of sittings suggests payment. Half-a-crown or 30 (old) pence was a typical fee for a half-day's modelling, at a time when unskilled female earnings averaged four pence an hour. It secured Lizzie a modest independence, at a period when family finances were straitened: her oldest brother Charles was sick. He died early in January 1852. As Millais told Hunt, this meant that 'Miss Siddall cannot sit to anyone for a fortnight.' That was a short mourning period: several months was deemed appropriate for a sibling. It suggests she was eager to return to the studios.

With normal courtesy, the artists addressed her as Miss Siddall. Between themselves, they called her 'Miss Sid' or 'The Sid', in emulation of French and Italian studio practice where 'La Susanna' or 'La Mignon' was a conventional appellation.

The now famous session in Millais' Gower Street studio, when she lay wearing a vintage ballgown in a tin bath of cooling water to simulate the drowning Ophelia, is a Pre-Raphaelite foundation myth—the foreshadowing of Elizabeth Siddal's fate, a figurative sacrifice to the movement, the female role as victim, near-death in the service of art.

More interestingly, perhaps, it testifies to Siddal's commitment, entering into the spirit of Millais's aim to recreate Ophelia's watery end. He was possibly a bit embarrassed afterwards, when the oil lamps warming the bath failed and Lizzie grew colder and colder. Although now celebrated, it was not widely spoken of at the time, and only the much-later recollection of fellow-artist Arthur Hughes secured its place in history. He wrote that Ophelia's appearance was 'wonderfully like' and that

> Miss Siddal had a trying experience while acting as a model for 'Ophelia'. In order that the artist might get the proper set of the garments in water and the right atmosphere and aqueous effects, she had to lie in large bath filled with water, which was kept at an even temperature by lamps placed beneath. One day, just as the picture was nearly finished, the lamps went out unnoticed by the artist, who was so intensely absorbed in his work that he thought of nothing else, and the poor lady was kept floating in the cold water till she was quite benumbed. She herself never complained of this, but the result was that she contracted a severe cold, and her father (an auctioneer at Oxford) wrote to Millais, threatening

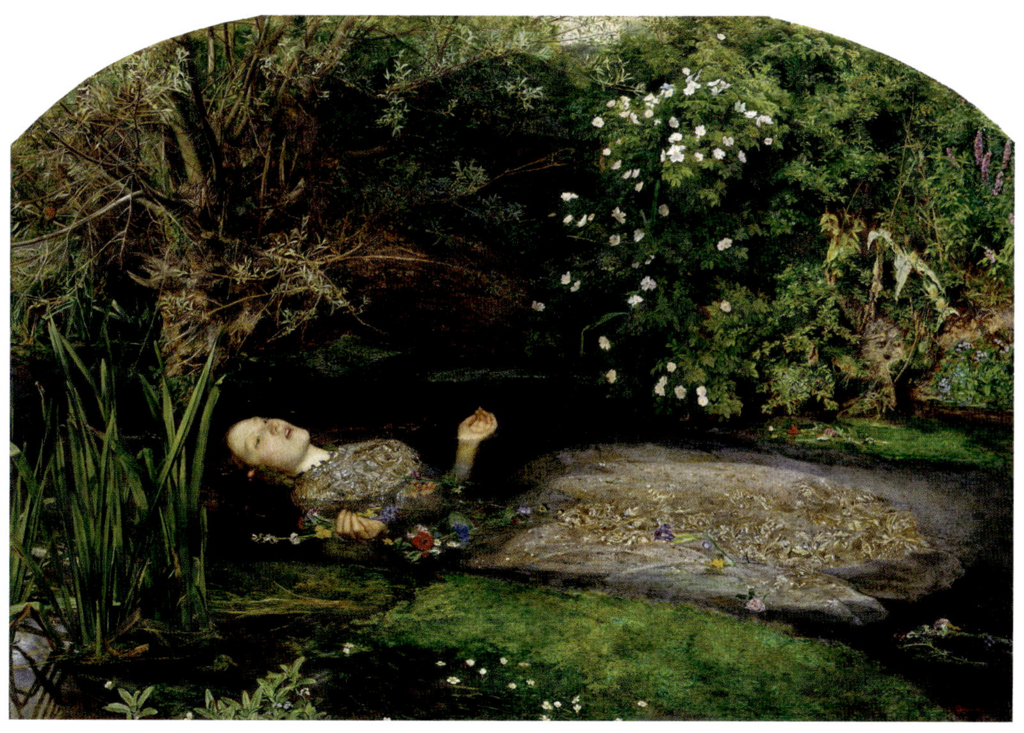

J. E. Millais, Ophelia, 1852

> him with an action for £50 damages for his carelessness. Eventually the matter was satisfactorily compromised. Millais paid the doctor's bill, and Miss Siddal, quickly recovering, was none the worse for her cold bath.[8]

Hughes continued with phrases about Millais's accurate rendering of Siddal's 'unworldly simplicity and purity of aspect', but his knowledge was faulty, because her father was not an auctioneer in Oxford or anywhere else (this was possibly a muddled allusion to Jane Burden's father, an Oxford stableman). One may also doubt the precise accuracy of alleged threat of legal action: although Millais may well have contributed towards

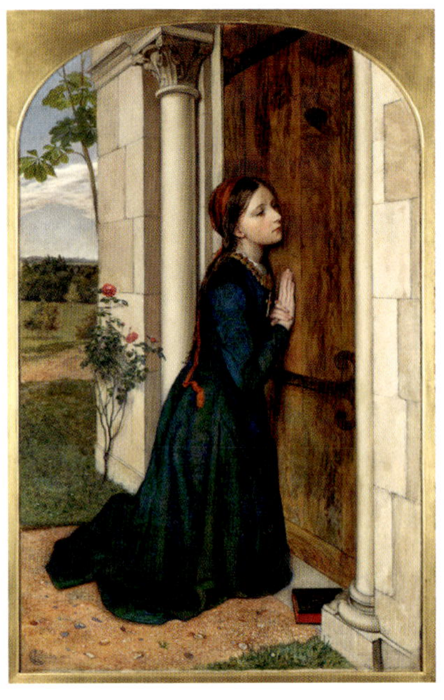

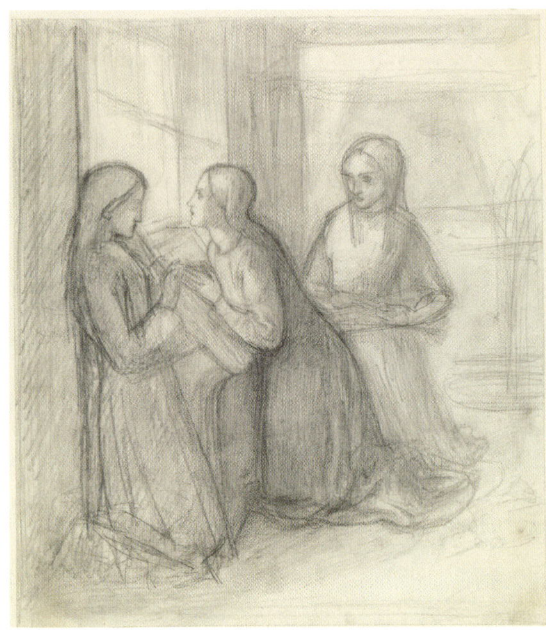

Left: C. A. Collins, The Devout Childhood of St Elizabeth of Hungary, 1851–2. This saint, who died in 1231, renounced her royal status to care for the poor and is venerated as a follower of St Francis of Assissi

Right: D. G. Rossetti, Study for St Elizabeth of Hungary and her Companions, 1852

a typical medical payment of one or two guineas, £50 was a huge claim (a workman's annual earnings). The key sentence is that Siddal 'never complained', and was clearly not deterred from modelling.

By 6 March the painting was done. It appears she then posed for Charley Collins, in another stressful pose, as the medieval St Elizabeth of Hungary kneeling outside a monastery door. Collins drew the saint as a teenager: as with Viola, Sylvia, Delia and Ophelia, as a model Siddal was like an actor, cast in various parts.

St Elizabeth was a popular subject at this moment, owing to pro- and anti-Catholic feeling, and to a controversial historical drama by Charles Kingsley, based on the saint's story of pious renunciation. In the spring of 1851, James Collinson, the original member of the PRB who on conversion to the Catholic faith resigned simultaneously from the Brotherhood and from his engagement to Christina Rossetti, exhibited his own picture of St Elizabeth, shown kneeling to kiss the feet of a crucified Christ. Gabriel Rossetti followed, showing the saint with two companions, where she is again kneeling and has Siddal's profile.

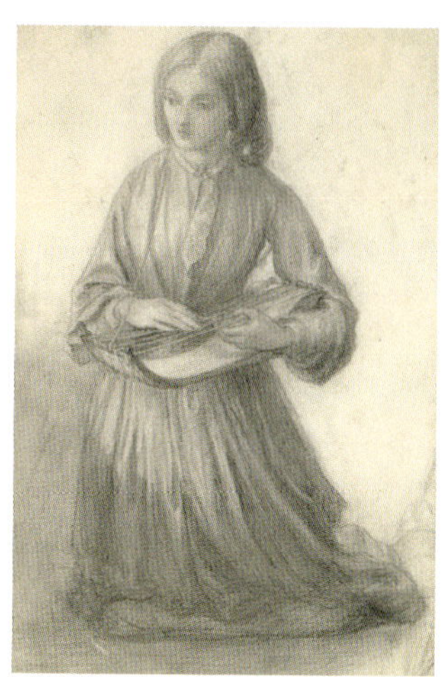

D. G. Rossetti, Study of Elizabeth Siddal with a Stringed Instrument, 1852

She posed also as female musicians, one with a stringed instrument, one blowing a double pipe. These were possibly drawn at the same time as her sessions with Collins, taking advantage of the kneeling pose. Romance began slowly that year.

In early summer 1852 Millais was painting near Bromley in Kent; Hunt was in Oxford and Sussex. Rossetti was without a studio of his own, so the graphic artist Edward Bateman, who was engaged to marry fellow artist Anna Mary Howitt, offered space in a garden cottage on the slopes of Highgate Hill. Known as the Nest, the cottage belonged to a house called the Hermitage, filled with antique furniture and china collected by Bateman.

Here, Gabriel worked on imaginative watercolour compositions featuring Dante and Beatrice, for which he used Siddal as model. In late May, the painter William Bell Scott, who was principal of the School of Design in Newcastle, arrived in London on his annual visit to the exhibitions. He turned up unannounced at the Nest one evening, to find himself 'face to face with Rossetti and a lady whom I did not recognise and could scarcely see. He did not introduce; she rose to go. I made a little bow, which she did not acknowledge; and she left.'[9] Later identifying the lady as 'Miss Siddal', Scott added disingenuously: 'Why he did not introduce us I cannot say [...] perhaps the maid should have called him instead of allowing me to invade the studio without warning.'

Perhaps a maidservant at the Hermitage did not know

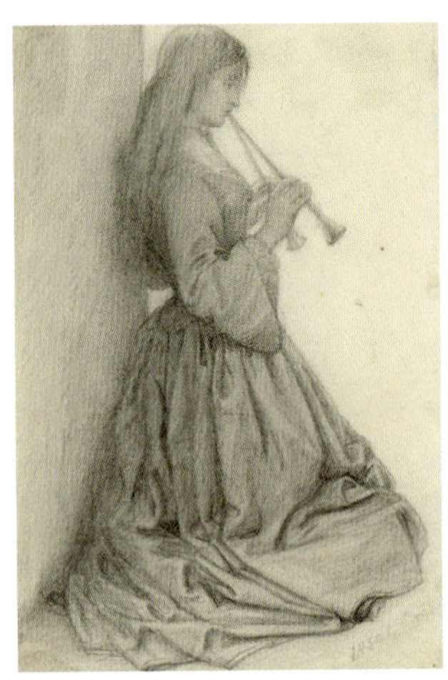

D. G. Rossetti, Study of Elizabeth Siddal with a Double Pipe, 1852

there was a visitor at the Nest. As a lady, Lizzie would have to explain her unchaperoned presence; as a model, she could remain anonymous, independent, and ambiguous. Now, with Gabriel, she was both modelling and drawing.

At some unknown date, she had revealed her own aspirations, and asked, or demanded, that they be considered. 'How truly she may say "No man cared for my soul,"' Gabriel told William Allingham,[10] explaining the transition from model to student.

And that's really the best verbal record of Siddal's ambition, alongside the obituary account told in Sheffield. This summer, with days spent together in a ramshackle garden studio, must mark the start of her relationship with Rossetti. Which is why non-verbal records—details of actions and travels and above all her artworks—are more eloquent than interpretations. Her general demeanour, as William Rossetti recalled in the 1890s, 'seemed to say "My mind and my feelings are my own, and no outsider is expected to pry into them."'[11]

Years later, Allingham offered his own recollections, remembering Siddal as 'sweet, gentle and kindly, and sympathetic to art and poetry', but not conventionally attractive. 'Her pale face, abundant red hair and long thin limbs were strange and affecting,' he wrote; 'never beautiful in my eyes'.[12]

It suited both Lizzie and Gabriel to be quite secretive. The cover version described her as his 'pupil'—a beginner training with an established artist. Successful painters took on pupils, like music students with a professional teacher. A decade later, Marie Spartali would study with Madox Brown in this manner. Of course, Siddal was not a regular, fee-paying pupil, but rather a model, whose posing would in theory pay for tuition. In addition, she was soon Gabriel's 'sweetheart'—in later language his girlfriend and unofficial fiancée.

She told Gabriel that she had nowhere to work at home except an unheated bedroom. Or he exaggerated her privations to increase her pathos. Certainly later commentators believed she lived in poverty.

Bateman sailed for Australia with William Howitt, whose family moved into the Hermitage; Anna Mary took over the Nest as her studio. Gabriel returned home. On 4 August, he wrote teasingly to his sister Christina, then visiting Staffordshire, asking for examples of her current sketches. 'You must take care not to rival the Sid,' he added, continuing in playful mode: 'I have had sent to me, among my things from Highgate, a lock of hair shorn from the beloved head of that dear, and radiant as the tresses of Aurora, a sight of which may perhaps dazzle you on your return.'[13] The inference is that Lizzie had snipped strands of her auburn hair, which Gabriel packed with other belongings as he returned home. This was vivid evidence of mutual affection that supports the terms 'beloved' and 'dear', even if these were rather undercut by the joking hyperbolic tone. We can note too, that Gabriel's siblings knew about Miss Siddal, although she had not been invited to meet the family. From his recollections, William Rossetti was as yet barely aware of her existence.

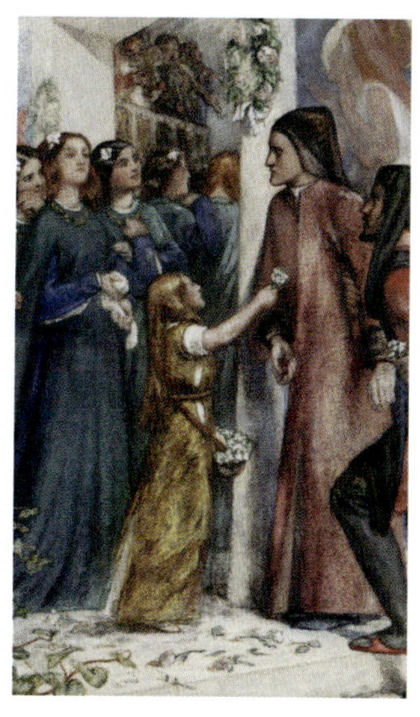

D. G. Rossetti, detail from The First Meeting of Dante and Beatrice, 1852. The subject, from Dante's Vita Nuova, shows Beatrice refusing to greet Dante when they meet in the street

So were they now definitely engaged? As if marking the event, Siddal made herself two new silk dresses, one grey that enhanced her appearance as 'a meek, unconscious dove', and one black that suggested an exotic black swan. These were more poeticisms from Gabriel. At the Nest, she had posed for figures of the Virgin and Beatrice in small compositions done in dry watercolour. One was exhibited at the end of the year; aptly it depicted the first meeting of Dante and Beatrice.[14] There are no surviving works of Siddal's own from this year, however.

The author of an early biography of Rossetti was told by someone that 'at Miss Siddall's request the engagement was not announced' and that 'its first publication to Rossetti's friends seems to have been contrary to her wishes'.[15] This sounds improbable, unless Gabriel himself was the anecdote's source. More likely the hesitation was on his part. Young men of his generation were warned to defer marriage, for wives typically produced children and the financial costs of supporting a family were heavy. Young artists were doubly warned that sexual acts depleted their creative energy. But possibly the reluctance was mutual: among the respectable middle classes, protocols applied to engaged couples—a weekend walk after church, decorous evenings at each family home, formal visits to other relatives. Lizzie did not enjoy such 'polite' performances.

They were certainly on first name terms—a distinct marker of relationship change. Gabriel now called her 'Lizzy' (his original spelling) and soon they were playfully using the mutual nickname 'Guggums', often shortened to 'Gug'. Their behaviour indicates that they intended to marry at a later date. Engagement custom decreed formal calls of presentation to both sets of parents and other relatives, but neither family was officially informed. This was not least because the Rossetti household was in financial and emotional crisis with their father's physical and mental incapacity. William had already been obliged to enter employment, in the Excise Office, his elder sister Maria took over her father's language teaching, Christina and their mother endeavoured to run a small school from home. By spring 1853 Mrs Rossetti moved herself, Christina and her husband to Somerset with similar aims. It was not opportune to introduce a prospective daughter-in-law. So only a few were told, notably Madox Brown.

Nonetheless, there was either a formal promise to marry or a shared understanding. Lizzie's willingness to accept a casual arrangement signals independence, as they assumed the (modest) freedoms accorded an engaged couple without open declaration. What did she tell her family? Following the death of her brother, the Siddalls were probably also in crisis. The dresses she made will have served mourning purposes through 1852–3, and the money that paid for both black and grey silk must have come from the family, unless she had saved earnings from modelling for Millais and Collins.

However, when towards the end of 1852, the latter asked her to sit again, she declined 'in a most freezing manner' saying she now had 'other occupation'.[16] Her modelling days were over.

What of the discovery in the bonnet shop? No other evidence that Siddal worked as a milliner exists. The story first appeared in Frederic Stephens' 1894 monograph on Rossetti, where Walter Deverell was credited with recruiting the 'tall, elegant, lithe, milliner's assistant' as a model. Holman Hunt followed this up in 1905 with his synoptic account of the moment 'when the name of Eleanor Siddal [as Hunt called her] was first heard in the studios'. Dramatizing the event, he recounted Deverell's excited announcement of spotting 'this stupendously beautiful creature' in the back room of a shop, adding that though her family was 'quite humble', she behaved 'liked a real lady'.[17] And so on.

Hunt's recollections were famously inventive by this date, and all other witnesses were dead. Nonetheless, the tale was repeated as a foundational PRB myth, though not believed by William Rossetti. It is now established as fact.

I prefer the version that Siddal met the Deverell family as a dressmaker and drew attention to her own drawings when offering to pose. Her story is not that of a Cinderella awaiting her prince, but of a resourceful Rosalind.

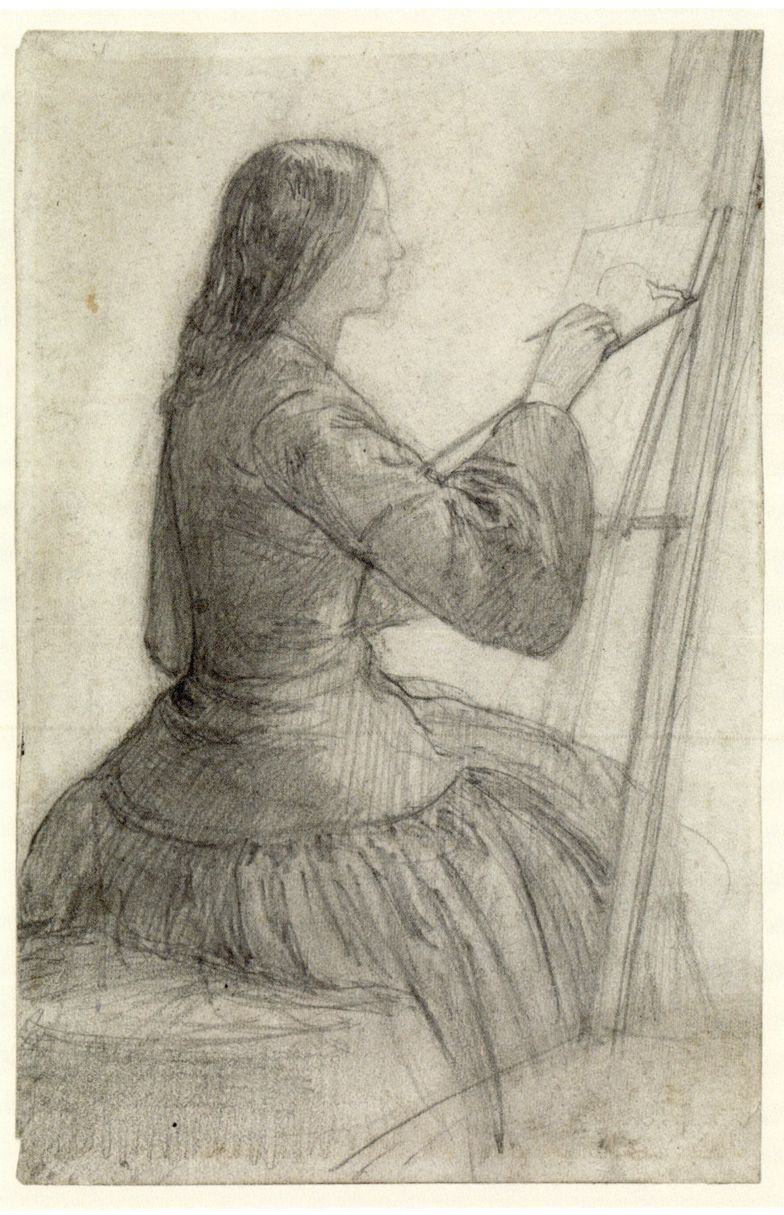

2. STUDIO

AT THE END OF 1852, Gabriel searched for a studio, looking in Highgate, Hornsey and Hampstead and then finding an apartment overlooking the Thames at Blackfriars. The rent was £60 a year, paid by William as co-tenant, though Gabriel was also in funds, selling three recent watercolours to fellow artists, which enabled him to pay for materials and purchase a new easel. A few weeks later he also received £50 for *Ecce Ancilla*, renamed as *The Annunciation*.

It's unclear how large the Chatham Place apartment was—at least two rooms, with perhaps a small bedroom where William and Gabriel shared a bed as they did at home. There was no kitchen, meals being bought in or supplied by the housekeeper from her basement realm, along with coals and hot water. Next to Blackfriars Bridge, it was within walking distance both of William's office near Charing Cross and of the Siddall home across the river in Southwark. As at the Nest, Lizzie could and did visit unchaperoned. Please would William stay away, Gabriel wrote one evening; Lizzie was coming and he did not 'of course wish anyone else to call'.[1] She did not move in, however, and it was more often a place for the fellows to gather, as on 2 December, when the Rossetti brothers played host to Hunt, Millais, Deverell, Fred Stephens and Tom Seddon. At the end of the month, Stephens was there again, with the sculptor Alex Munro, the painters Arthur Hughes and Henry Wells, the glass designer John Clayton and the landscapist George Boyce, whose diary records 'roast chestnuts and coffee, honey, hot spirits' and 'delightful' conversation in 'gentlemanly' company.[2] No mention of Miss Siddal.

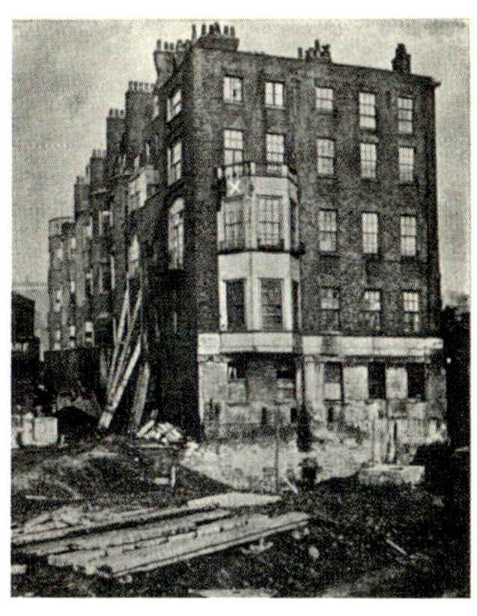

Chatham Place, Blackfriars, London, shortly before demolition. Rossetti's apartment was above the double-storey bay, overlooking the Thames

Opposite: D. G. Rossetti, Study of Elizabeth Siddal at the Easel, c. 1854–5. Holding a crayon, her right hand is steadied by resting on an artist's mahlstick

Henceforth, Siddal's history has always been so closely entwined with Rossetti's that her independent life is hard to trace. Most of those who knew her recorded only what they recalled about her role as Rossetti's inamorata.

The author Mary Howitt recalled seeing 'a good deal of

Miss Siddall' after the Howitts moved into the Hermitage, but was unimpressed by her artwork, 'for what she produced had no originality to it'.[3] Howitt's niece, living near Epping, remembered a picnic when her cousin Anna Mary visited with Rossetti and Siddal, the former loquaciously 'in rattling good spirits', the latter mostly silent.[4] As a serious female artist, who had studied in London and Munich, Anna Mary provided Siddal with a role model. 'Oh! How terribly did I long to be a man in order to paint there,' she wrote after a brief visit to the Royal Academy Schools. 'I felt quite angry at being a woman, it seemed to me such a mistake.'[5] As well as publishing an account of her time in Bavaria, Howitt also wrote a story about a possible 'art sisterhood' to emulate the PRB.

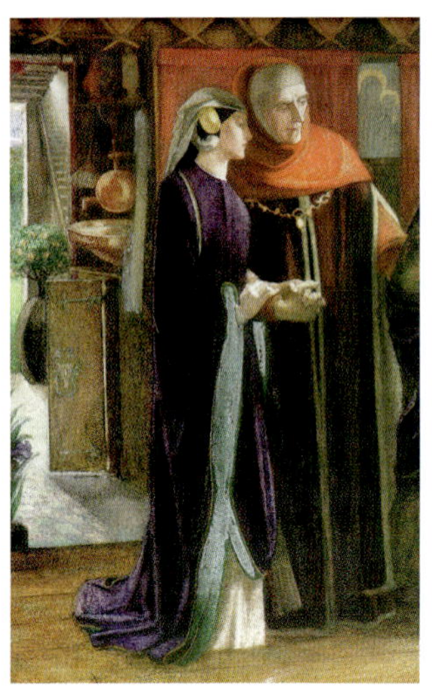

D. G. Rossetti, detail from The First Anniversary of Beatrice's Death, 1853. Also from the Vita Nuova, this scene shows Siddal as one of the visitors who interrupted Dante's reverie

Another new acquaintance was young Emma Hill, who in April 1853 married Madox Brown, at the church of St Dunstan-in-the-East. Gabriel was a witness, also lending his rooms for a wedding breakfast. Siddal's presence is not recorded, but she had already met Ford, Emma, and their two-year-old daughter Cathy. I've conjectured elsewhere that the famous nickname 'Guggums' came from Cathy's infant attempt at 'Gabriel', briefly applied to both him and Lizzie, and taken up by them in mutual affection. But there was no opportunity to meet Gabriel's parents, as they were in Somerset, hoping a quieter life would benefit Professor Rossetti's frail health.

On the days that she went to Gabriel's studio, Siddal could walk from Kent Place carrying her small portfolio to the Elephant and Castle junction, then north along Blackfriars Road to the bridge and across to Chatham Place. She was studying with some seriousness. In January 1853 she and Gabriel visited the first photographic exhibition to be held in London, and at another date they looked at medieval illustrations in the manuscript collections of the British Museum—either in the library there, or in reproduction. They were reading Robert Browning's dramatic poems. Gabriel was working on a scene from Dante's *Vita Nuova*, for which she posed for a full-length figure, and she herself was illustrating Tennyson's ballad 'The Lady of Shalott'—not then as famous as it became.

Drawing on his rather thin memories of Siddal, Arthur Hughes later wrote:

> She had read Tennyson, having first come to know something about him by finding one or two of his poems on a piece of paper which she brought home to her mother wrapped round a pat of butter. Rossetti taught her to draw, she used to be drawing while sitting to him.[6]

The Shalott line drawing was both careful and bold, placing a stiff figure seated at an upright tapestry loom, awkwardly twisting towards a wide window. To left, a small image of a mounted knight is reflected in a large mirror that has spider-web cracks, and the threads of the tapestry fly apart as if in a gale.

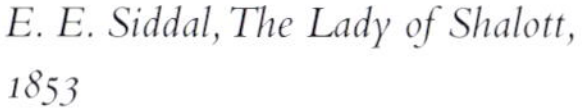

E. E. Siddal, The Lady of Shalott, 1853

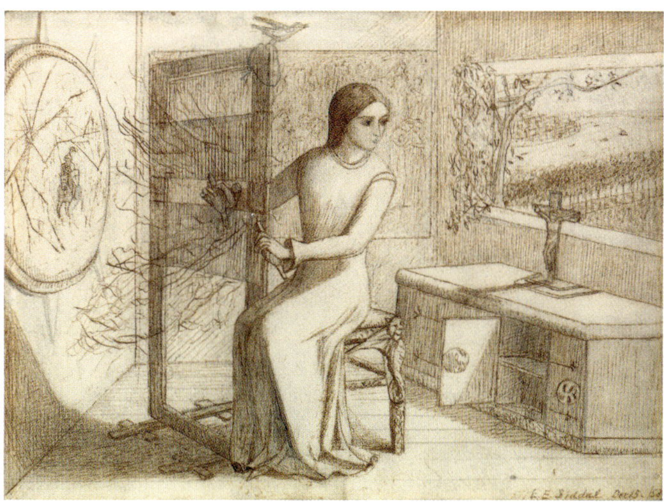

The narrative: by disobediently turning to look, the Lady triggers the curse that leads to her death. This key action in the poem was also depicted by Holman Hunt in a drawing in 1850, which Siddal probably saw; if so she borrowed only the Lady's hairstyle and features for her own ambitious composition. Her draughtsmanship is naïve, but the elements are studied. The perspective is defined, if not quite accurate, the drapery of the lady's gown convinces and the shadows cast by figure, loom and furniture are well depicted. The turning posture and flying threads convey dramatic movement, though the Lady's expression is rather calm; she seems more in control of the fateful moment than the poem allows. If this is in some sense a self-image—as so many post-Romantic artworks are—it presents a decisive moment in action, and the drawing itself is Siddal's new occupation. She has challenged social prescriptions in favour of an unknown future.

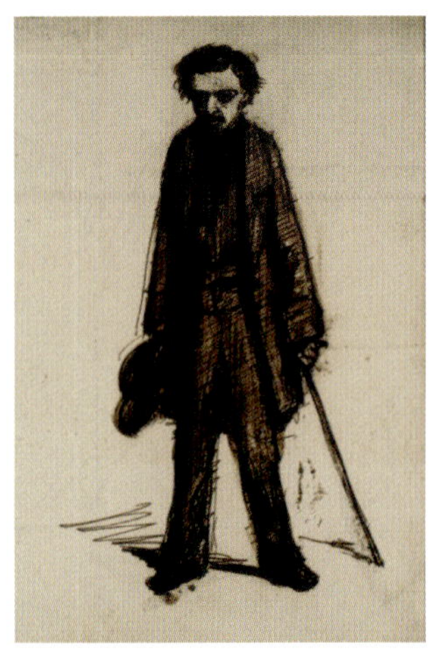

D. G. Rossetti, Self-caricature, showing his typically dishevelled appearance, 1853

She signed the drawing 'E. E. Siddal', in a professional manner. It was fashionable in the PRB generation to devise distinctive monograms—Rossetti tried out several over the years—but she relied on the simpler signature. Much has been made of the spelling, given that the commonest usage was 'Siddall'; but both versions are seen for example in the census returns compiled by enumerators. Lizzie may have followed her parents in choosing 'Siddal', or perhaps because this looked more refined. Class anxiety was highly attuned. Possibly, the PRBs used this version without knowing of an alternative, and that she then liked to adopt it, as a mark of artistic identity. I haven't seen any confirmation of the assertion that Rossetti chose it for her.

When in July Gabriel left London, going first to Newcastle and then Stratford-on-Avon, he sent an urgent message to William. 'I want to tell you that Lizzy is painting at Blackfriars,' he wrote. 'Do not therefore encourage anyone to go near the

E. E. Siddal, Self-Portrait, 1853-4

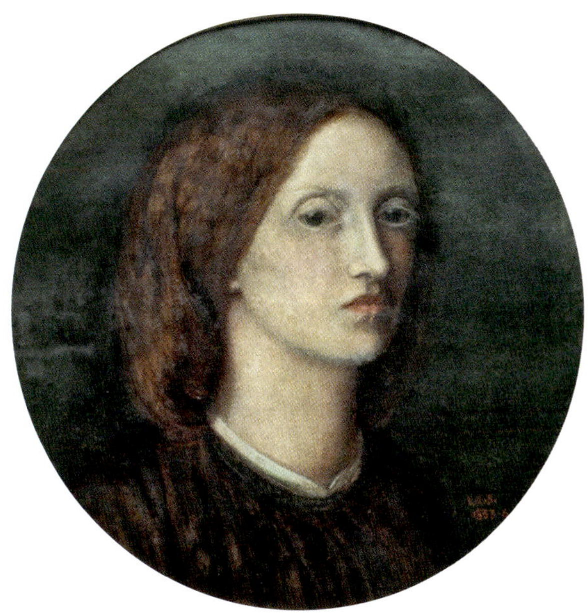

place. I have told her to keep the doors locked, and she will probably sleep there sometimes.'[7] This was another bold move, signalling her independent spirit which would have been scandalous if known. Using his paints, she was engaged on a small, circular self-portrait, a typical student's assignment (chiefly because the model is always available) but difficult to one not practised in handling oils. It also requires the deft use of a mirror, with the reflection at a steady angle in the same, sustained light. The result was a strong, unglamourised likeness, showing a three-quarter face with pinched, almost severe features, hooded eyelids and a red-head's pale lashes.

Remarkably accomplished for a beginner, it is fully Pre-Raphaelite in its frank realism, with no hint of the coy pose and simpering expression common in contemporary female portraiture. With lifted chin, attitude and gaze are assured and confident, the expression even assertive, although more likely the effect of prolonged observation. And with chestnut hair loosely looped up, the subject presents a simple, unadorned appearance, wearing a plain dark dress with a narrow collar that emphasises the long tall neck. All is offset by the rich green background.

Sadly, the location of this fine artwork is currently unknown. It was last seen around 1970 in Oxford, having passed to William Rossetti's descendants. When it is re-discovered, it will provide excellent scope for assessing Siddal's skill at this date, as well as more discussion of her self-presentation.

'Lizzy has made a perfect wonder of her portrait, which is nearly done,' Brown was told when Gabriel returned to London. It would be sent to the winter exhibition. Moreover, she was about to begin work on a new picture, destined for the next year's Academy summer show.[8] Neither happened.

Her earnest endeavour is caught in a vigorous thumbnail sketch that Rossetti made in September, showing Siddal leaning over a drawing board to sketch himself perched uncomfortably on an upright chair—the role-reversal of artist and model. It is vivid evidence of her artistic determination, and is not flattering. At this period most images of women at the easel convey graceful femininity, in the same manner as when shown sewing or piano-playing.

Naturally, she could adopt such poses when required. But her own drawings indicate resolution. *The Lady of Shalott* is neatly dated 'Dec 15/53'. It was succeeded within a month by work on a composition of *We Are Seven*, illustrating Wordsworth's poem. Though the picture is currently unlocated, a vintage photograph shows a cottage girl amidst gravestones, with church, lake and mountains behind.

What do Siddal's subject choices suggest? A Romantically pathetic poem, 'We Are Seven' invokes defiance as well as pathos,

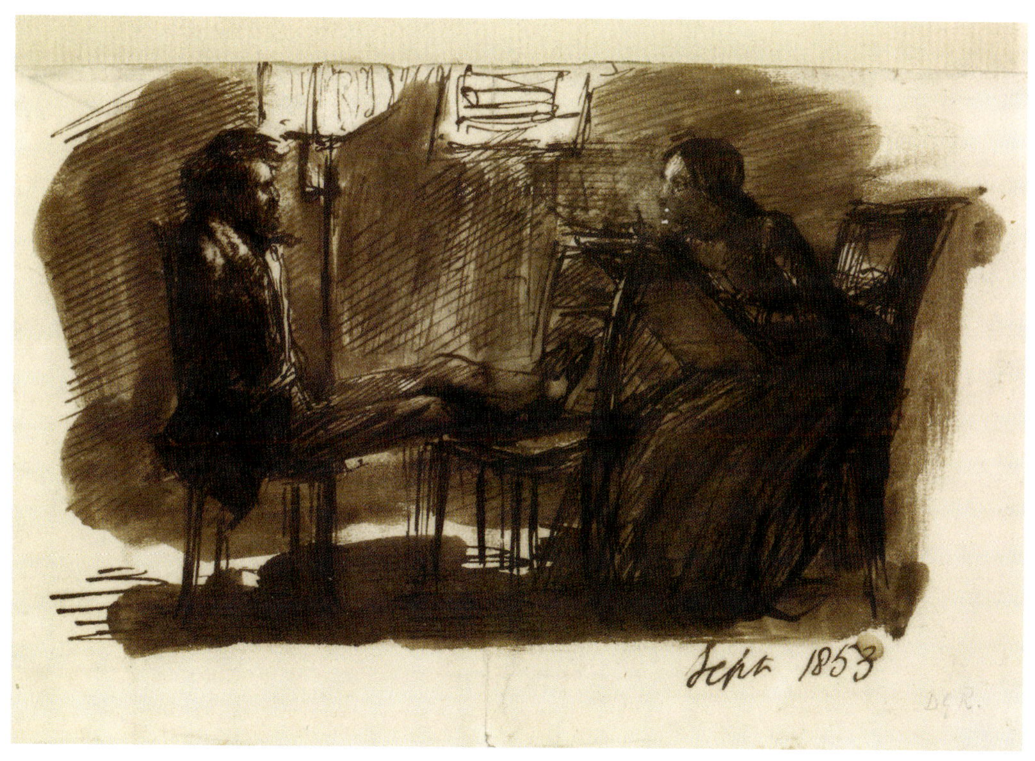

D. G. Rossetti, Caricature of Himself Posing at Chatham Place for Siddal to Draw his Portrait, 1853

the girl asserting that her six buried siblings nevertheless 'are'. Poignantly, too, the death of Lizzie's brother Charles had reduced the Siddall brothers and sisters from seven to six. The Shalott ballad is open to interpretation, but the Lady's action is avowedly transgressive. Both attest to the artist's feeling for poetry, which antedated her introduction to the artworld.

'Pippa Passes', her next subject, speaks to Rossetti's influence, as he was a vigorous admirer of Robert Browning's dramatic dialogues at a time when the poet was deemed 'difficult' and unpopular. 'Pippa Passes' unfolds an early Renaissance

E. E. Siddal, *Pippa Passes*, 1853

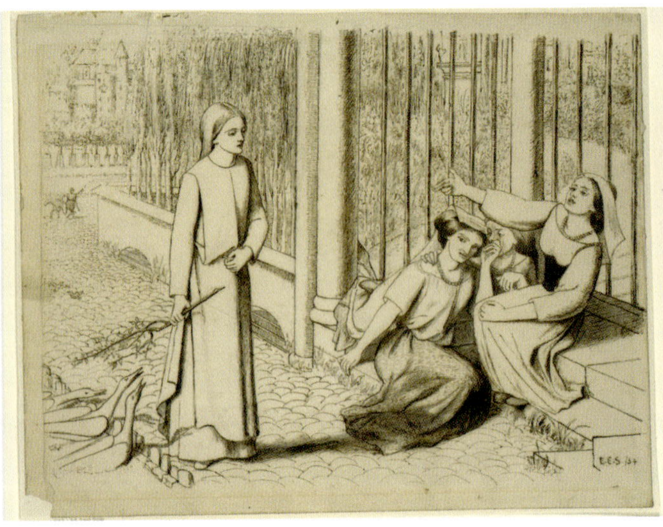

day in the life of a girl in Asolo, Italy, walking through the town, as various incidents occur, including plots to murder an elderly husband and assassinate an imperial officer. Political, personal and sexual wrongdoing interweave during warm spring weather. (The poem is also notorious for Browning's misuse of the word 't★★t' to mean a nun's headwear or coif.)

In a confident line drawing,[9] Siddal chose a scene where the virginal Pippa encounters three 'loose women' or courtesans, gossiping about their lovers. A bold theme for a female artist to choose, although her new friend Anna Mary Howitt depicted comparable 'fallen women' in paintings of Margaret seduced by Faust, and *The Castaway,* showing a desolate flower girl with her illegitimate child, mired in 'dust and ashes'. This image was described as 'strong-minded'—that is, a controversial artistic protest against social ostracism.

'Lizzie sits by me at work on her design, which is now

coming really admirable,' Gabriel told Brown in January 1854. 'She has also finished the "Lady of Shalott" sketch [and] followed your suggestion about her portrait and done several things, which improve it greatly.'[10] One would love to know what advice Brown offered. It is clear that work on the self-portrait continued for some time, as the likeness was painstakingly built up and refined.

By this date, the relationship was acknowledged to Gabriel's family, who in March 1854 regrouped in London. As his father was now dying, Lizzie met only Christina, whom he invited to call when Lizzie would be at Chatham Place. He would be glad if Christina came to see Lizzie's drawings, Gabriel told William, 'as I have told Lizzie she mentioned her wish to do so'. Both women were probably quite shy—customarily, a fiancée was formally introduced to all family members, but these were irregular circumstances. One evening, Rossetti and Allingham also escorted Christina and Lizzie to meet the Howitts at the Hermitage. 'Not fair as men would reckon fair, Nor noble as they count the line', Christina wrote in a poem. 'Only as graceful as a bough And tendrils of the vine.' If this was based on Siddal, she behaved with extreme modesty:

> And down cast were her dovelike eyes
> And downcast was her tender cheek,
> Her pulses fluttered like a dove
> To hear him speak.

With typical eagerness, Gabriel proposed a collaboration, for Lizzie to illustrate his sister's verses. A month later their father died, curtailing all social activity for the Rossetti women.

Mrs Howitt, who with apparent good intention perceived Siddal to be 'very unwell', recommended the homeopath Garth Wilkinson. A favoured alternative practitioner, he diagnosed 'curvature of the spine' or scoliosis, for which there was no evidence, and said she should stop painting. Of course she would continue, reported Rossetti; she was at that moment working 'on the most poetical of all possible designs,' probably the Wordsworthian scene.[11]

Miss Howitt and her feminist friend Barbara Smith were rather taken with the romance between young Mr Rossetti and a shopkeeper's daughter. Or perhaps they were most taken by the young Mr Rossetti, with his revolutionary antecedents and artistic originality (they had read *The Germ* in 1850, responding to its 'true feeling' and search for simplicity).[12] They resolved to befriend his sweetheart, commending a sanatorium run by Barbara's cousin Florence Nightingale. Barbara wrote a breathless letter to a third friend, Bessie Parkes:

> Private now my dear I have got a strong interest in a young girl formerly a model to Millais and Dante Rossetti now Rossetti's love and pupil, she is a genius and will (if she lives) be a great artist, her gift discovered by a strange accident such as rarely befall woman. Alas! Her whole life has been hard and full of trials, her home unhappy and her whole fate hard. Rossetti has been an honourable friend to her and I do not doubt if circumstances were favourable would marry her. She is of course under a ban having been a model (tho' only to 2 PRBs).[13]

This is the earliest surviving account of Siddal's origins as a Cinderella tale. A second note continued:

> I think Miss S. is a genius and is very beautiful and although she is not a lady her mind is poetic and that D. Rossetti sympathises and does not much consider the 1st. He wishes her to see Ladies and it seems to me the only way to keep her self-esteem from sinking as I do not think

she will recover and perhaps that prevents one from thinking too much about the future for them.

These thoughts eloquently reveal Siddal's social standing, and Rossetti's presentation of her position. A model could not be a suitable wife for a gentleman and in any case she was not 'a lady'. In this situation, what future awaited the couple? (Possibly one like Barbara's parents, who were not married despite many children, and therefore shunned by their wealthy father's relatives; Barbara did not wish to pursue this topic.)

Siddal declined hospital treatment, but agreed to a health-giving holiday in Hastings, with clean sea air in place of the polluted London atmosphere, worsened this year by outbreaks of water-borne cholera. Bessie Parkes secured lodgings in a cottage for three months from Easter, and Lizzie and Gabriel took separate rooms, he having to return to London for his father's funeral. It was customary for London artists to spend summer months away from London sketching or travelling, so this fell within a professional framework for Siddal's new life, despite being always presented in terms of ill-health. She did in fact send to Wilkinson via Gabriel a list of her symptoms, which led to a referral to a local homeopathic practitioner, whom she consulted; his verdict was that the 'very greatest care' was required.[14]

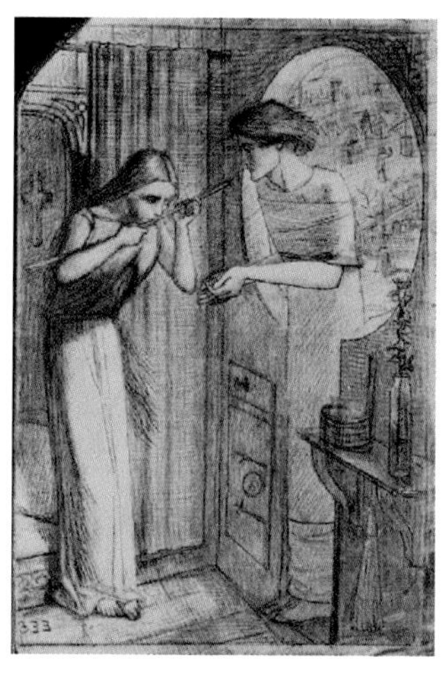

E. E. Siddal, Study for Clerk Saunders, 1854. May Margaret re-affirms her vows, as the ghost of her murdered lover, still wrapped in his shroud, materialises through the castle wall

A new project had recently been aired when Siddal met Irish poet William Allingham, who settled briefly in London. She and Gabriel were 'to illustrate the old Scottish ballads which Allingham is editing for Routledge,' Rossetti told Brown. 'She has just done her first block (from *Clerk Saunders*) and it is lovely. Her power of designing even increases greatly, and her fecundity of invention & facility are quite wonderful, much greater than mine.'[15]

Thus, in the 18 months since she had renounced modelling, she had substantial artistic achievements. She was, however,

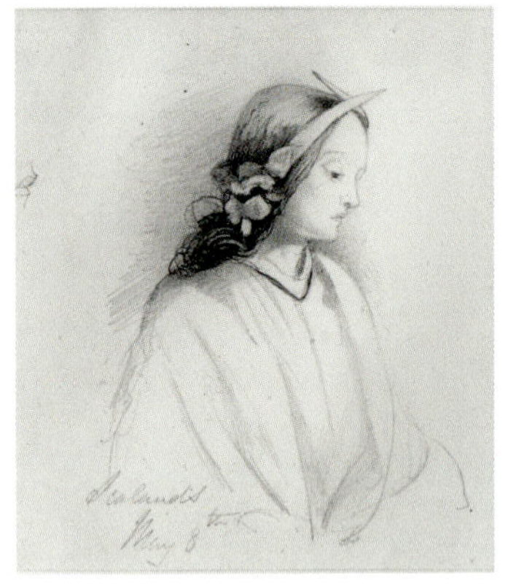

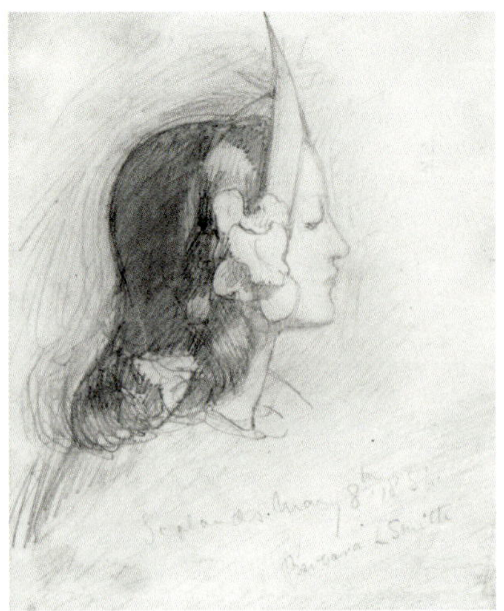

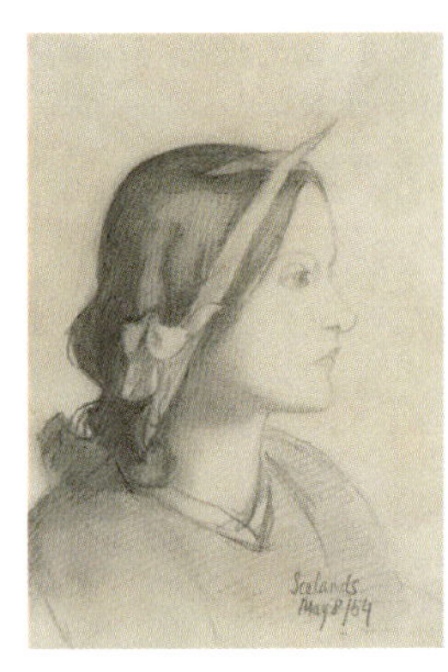

Three studies of Elizabeth Siddal drawn on the same day, 8 May 1854, when she posed at Scalands, Sussex, with wild iris pinned in her hair. Left to right: by Anna Mary Howitt, Barbara Leigh Smith (later Bodichon) and D. G. Rossetti

As Scalands the women got Lizzie to pose with wild irises pinned to her hair, as if she were a model. The results reflect differing presentations: Howitt depicted a modest, downcast aspect, Barbara a prouder head-held-high with disdainful gaze, and Rossetti a fully alert profile view, with an aspect of youthful innocence.

Artists customarily sat to each other, but on this occasion Siddal was not invited to take her turn drawing her companions. She was, however, sketching out of doors. The landscape behind the as-yet-untitled *Lovers Listening to Music* suggests the Sussex coast near a site known as Lovers' Seat. Although many sketches and studies are lost, the photographic record also includes a figure study that could relate to Rossetti's description of a 'dark gipsy-looking girl of about thirteen', with a 'very fine baby sister', whom Siddal brought to their lodgings as models. She was busy with ideas for the Border ballads book, having acquired a copy of Walter Scott's anthology *Minstrelsy of the Scottish Border*.[18]

As well as 'Clerk Saunders', she had visual ideas for 'The Maid of Loch Royan', 'The Gay Goshawk' and 'Sir Patrick Spens', where the group of ladies watch in vain from low green cliffs for their lords' return from Norroway o'er the sea. All four compositions were sketched out at Hastings.[19]

One must admit that ambition out-ran expertise, for in technical terms Siddal's drawing was tentative, her figures boneless, the spatial values weak. She did not often draw from observation, had no understanding of anatomy and little skill in modelling volumes through shading, all of which were basic to art training. But the Pre-Raphaelites valorised concept over correctness, and Siddal's actions in this period are those of a serious student. It is at the same time clear that she and Gabriel were in love, and foresaw (inasmuch as they did foresee further than the present) a shared life. This may be inferred as an artistic partnership such as Anna Howitt had envisioned with Edward

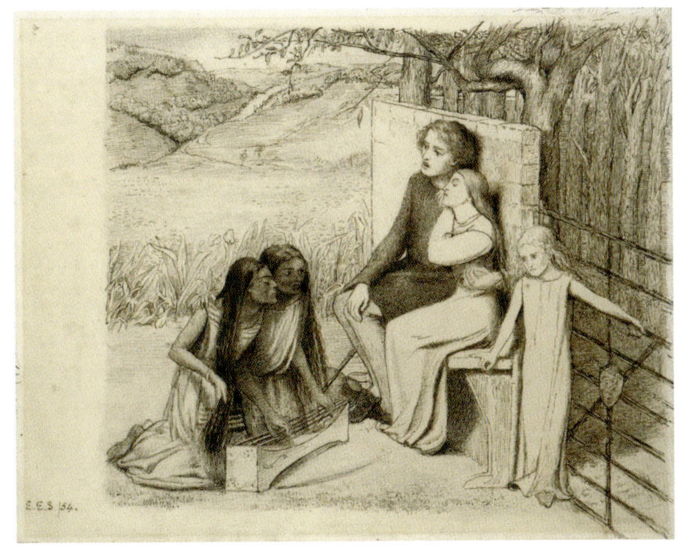

E. E. Siddal, Lovers Listening to Music, 1854. The landscape here is similar to that near Hastings, but the subject (and correct title) is unknown. The musicians may evoke the Abyssinian damsel playing on a dulcimer in Coleridge's vision of Kubla Khan, or the teams of Indian and Romany street entertainers in Victorian Britain

Bateman, or Henry Wells was currently planning for himself and Joanna Boyce.

A glimpse of collaboration is seen in Siddal's illustrative sketches for Rossetti's ballad-style poem 'Sister Helen', which Mrs Howitt had taken for magazine publication; here the story-line echoes the theme of transgression, as the heroine melts a wax figure of the faithless lover whom her young brother watches riding to his death. The Gothick theme was to her taste, and several compositional studies were made.

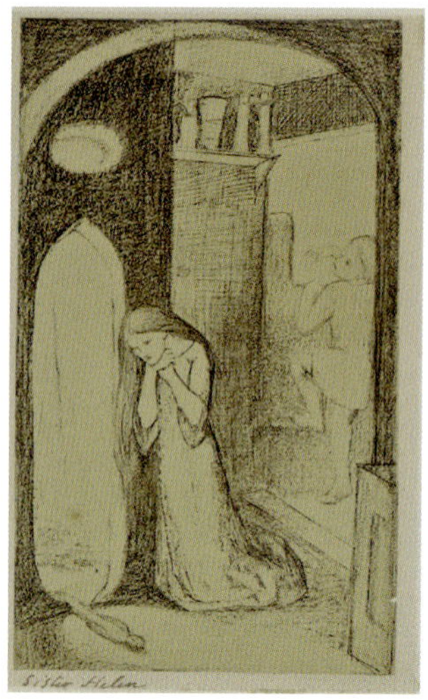

E. E. Siddal, Sketch illustrating Rossetti's poem 'Sister Helen', date unknown

During these Hastings weeks, they were continuously together both outdoors and in, unlike a typical engaged couple with far more formal lives. Explaining their lodgings, Gabriel assured his mother there was nothing improper about joining Lizzie in her room during the day—adding that both Miss Smith and Miss Parkes agreed. But it was decidedly irregular: Lizzie took the risk that she be judged 'not a lady'. The 'attitude of reserve' and distance was her defiance against such slurs. To this was added an air of frailty, for ladies were held to have delicate health.

Something significant seems to have happened during one of their walks together. The weather at Hastings was first cool and windy, then warm and windless; from the shore the becalmed fishing boats with their black sails looked like flies on a window blind. One day there was a thunderstorm, recalled by Rossetti in a poem where 'as in the wood that day', the lovers were 'one with the other all alone; And we were blithe.'

In that hour, as 'dull raindrops' heralded thunder, the poet 'won strength For words'. That evening 'I spoke those words again Beside the pelted window pane; And there she hearkened what I said.' Henceforth, it appears they were committed to each other. Another poem compared the beloved to 'my life's own sister well enough!'

'Love floated on the mists of morn And rested on the sunset's rays', Siddal wrote in a poem of her own:

Love held me joyful through the day
And streaming ever through the night:
No evil thing could come to me,
My spirit was so light.

Other verses invoke 'the day when we two stood Beneath the clinging trees in that dark wood'.

When Barbara Smith argued again for the Nightingale sanatorium, Gabriel replied on Lizzie's behalf. She had prepared a design that was 'practicable' for her to paint in his studio, because she wished to make real progress and 'set her mind a little more at ease about her pursuit of art'. Practice, he wrote, would bring more health than bed rest.[20]

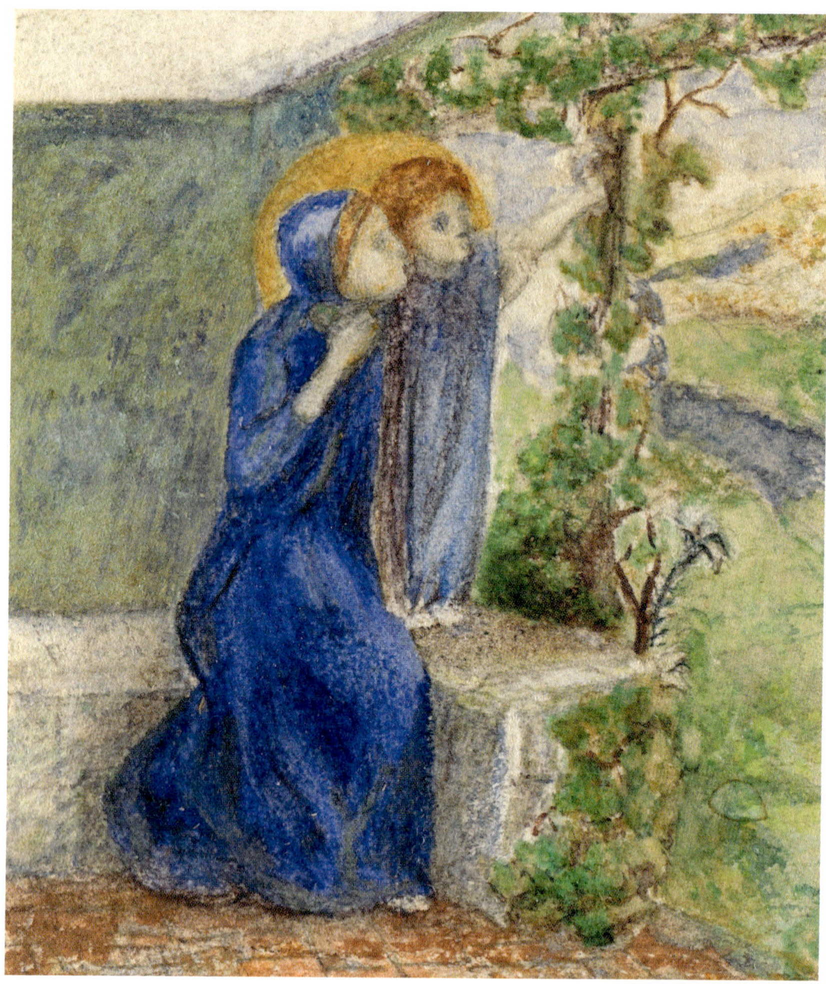

3. RUSKIN

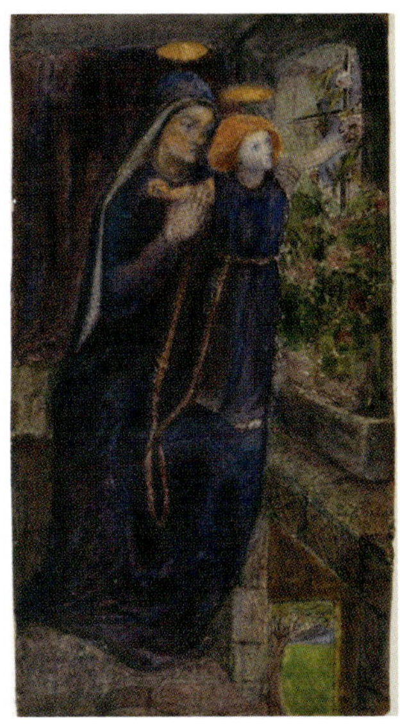

E. E. Siddal, Madonna and Christ Child, c. 1855

Opposite: E. E. Siddal, Madonna and Christ Child, c. 1855 (approximately twice actual size)

RETURNING TO LONDON at the end of June 1854, Siddal set to work. Allingham returned to Ireland, so the ballad book hung fire, and her designs were now for watercolours, not engravings. One contained a red-haired Christ Child standing on the Madonna's lap. Though clothed, the energetic Child is not dissimilar to the vigorous, curly haired infant in the *sacra conversazione* by Andrea del Sarto, an early acquisition by the National Gallery that Siddal may well have seen.

Two versions of this subject reveal her approach. One is set outdoors, in a sort of pergola with landscape beyond, the other by a window within a masonry building. In the outdoor image, both heads in one aureole; indoors, each has a hovering halo. Her painting equipment included pencils, crayons, brushes, pigment cakes known as 'moist colours', books or blocks of thick paper, and also erasers, for the opaque watercolour technique they used allowed for passages to be rubbed or scraped out and redrawn. Too much scraping could create a hole in the paper, to be patched from the back.

The Nativity was another projected subject, for which several sketches exist, showing the Virgin Mary and Christ Child in the stable, with a manger that is more like a table and a roughly delineated ox and ass in two of the designs. They show she was practising perspective as well as figure drawing. The devotional subjects were artistic staples to which the PRB had given renewed currency. Holman Hunt was painting Christ as the Light of the World, Rossetti was intermittently working on the Life of the Virgin.

It is anachronistic to suppose that Siddal aimed for a creative career as her counterpart might do today. Like all Victorian women, her goal was economic security which, without a wealthy family, meant marriage. Usually, however, marriage also entailed relinquishing other ambitions, displaced by duties to husband, housekeeping and children. Having secured a promise of marriage, Siddal evidently intended to continue painting. Long engagements were customary. Although the Browns repeatedly urged marriage, Lizzie seems to have chiefly demanded confirmation of the commitment, not an immediate move to a conjugal home.

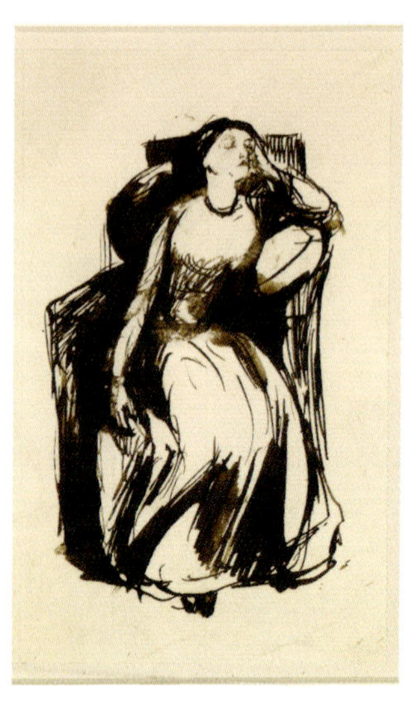

D. G. Rossetti, Study of Elizabeth Siddal Asleep in a Chair, date unknown

Writing to Allingham a month later, Rossetti described their relationship in fanciful terms of a rescue mission, with aspects based on her supposed frailty:

> It seems hard to me when I look at her sometimes, working or too ill to work, and think how many without one tithe of her genius or greatness of spirit have granted them abundant health, and opportunity, while perhaps her soul is never to bloom nor her bright hair to fade, but after hardly escaping from degradation and corruption, all she might have been must sink out again unprofitably in that dark house where she was born. How truly she may say 'No man cared for my soul'. I do not mean to make myself an exception, for how long have I known her, and not thought of this till so late—perhaps too late.

He assured Allingham it was 'the nearest thing to my own heart'.[1]

Siddal is unlikely to have shared the assessment of her 'genius' and 'greatness of spirit', but it fostered the Romantic notion of untutored brilliance hiding unexpectedly in low places. And although a cynical contemporary might have suspected ill health was a means to secure a lover's sympathy, it is also a fact that being 'unwell' commonly referred with dismaying frequency to monthly periods, perhaps concealed from Rossetti during the weeks in Hastings. Calling at the end of October, Brown endorsed both frailty and genius, noting that she looked 'thinner and more deathlike and more beautiful and

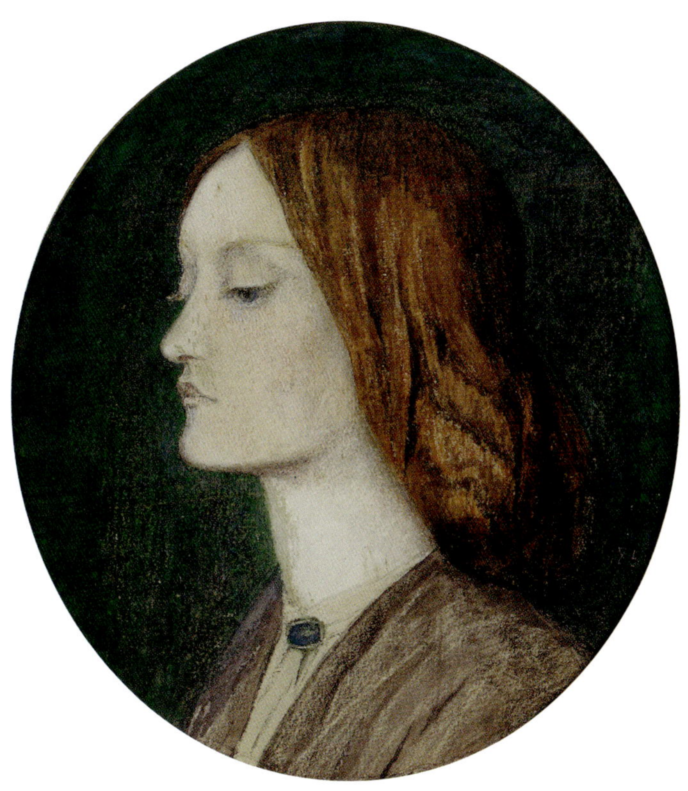

D. G. Rossetti, Elizabeth Siddal, c. 1855

more ragged than ever,' and was 'a real artist, a woman without parallel for many a long year'.[2]

Rossetti emulated her resolve, getting started on his own 'fallen woman' picture, to be entitled *Found*, in which a countryman discovers his former sweetheart morally degraded in the city street. Taking the canvas, he lodged with the Browns in Finchley, painting a local calf with Pre-Raphaelite precision. Siddal had a key to his apartment, so when Gabriel asked William to get tickets for a lecture by John Ruskin, they were to be sent 'to Lizzie at my place'. She should invite Anna Howitt and Barbara Smith.

The ballad book project lapsed, all woodblock designs abandoned apart from *Clerk Saunders,* transferred to watercolour. Over the winter of 1854–5 Rossetti cultivated Ruskin as a source of patronage for them both. When the critic returned to Britain after his summer travels in Europe, he was without protégés. Millais had abruptly severed all contact now he was intending to marry Ruskin's former wife Effie, and Hunt was far away. Rossetti was well placed to benefit. Firstly, Gabriel volunteered to teach at the new Working Men's College, where Ruskin was enthusiastically planning evening classes for 'sign painters and shop decorators and brickmakers and glassblowers'. Ruskin was also writing *The Stones of Venice*, promoting Gothic and medieval modes in place of neo-classicism. He bought Gabriel's small, medievalish image of a girl playing a lute, and supplied a list of subjects he would commission, though warning that his father's strict business habits did not permit payment in advance. Lizzie obligingly posed for two of Ruskin's subjects—Rachel and Leah, and Passover in the Holy Family.

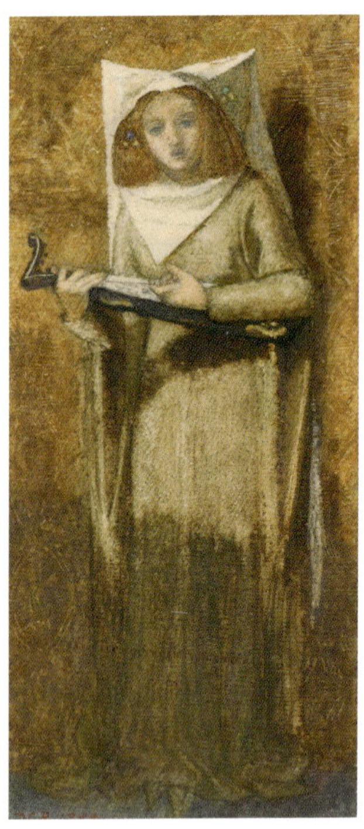

D. G. Rossetti, Girl Singing to a Lute, 1853

She too was productive. 'She is now doing two lovely watercolours,' Rossetti told Ruskin on 23 January 1855. One was the 'We Are Seven' illustration to Wordsworth, now worked up in colour, the other Keats' fantasy ballad, 'La Belle Dame sans Merci', which is known from sketches only. Reinforcing the need for patronage, he added that previously Siddal had 'found herself always thrown back for lack of health and wealth in the attempts she had made to begin a picture.'[3]

Of the two, wealth was most required; but benefactors were more sympathetic to illness.

This approach was followed up in March, when Rossetti showed Siddal's drawings to Ruskin, explaining that her family did not support her aspirations. Mr Siddal, he added, was a watchmaker, and her health was precarious. Philanthropically,

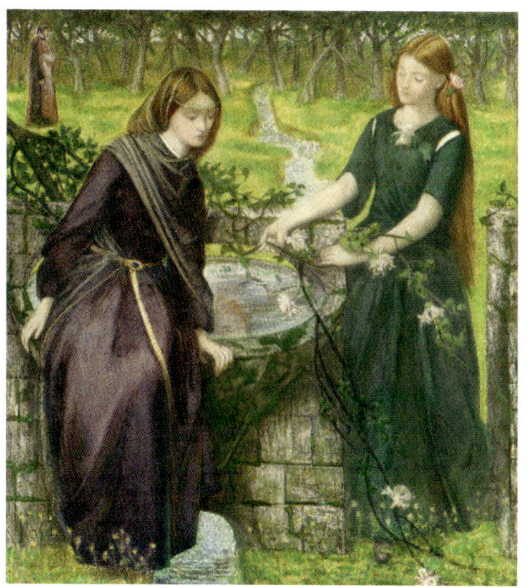

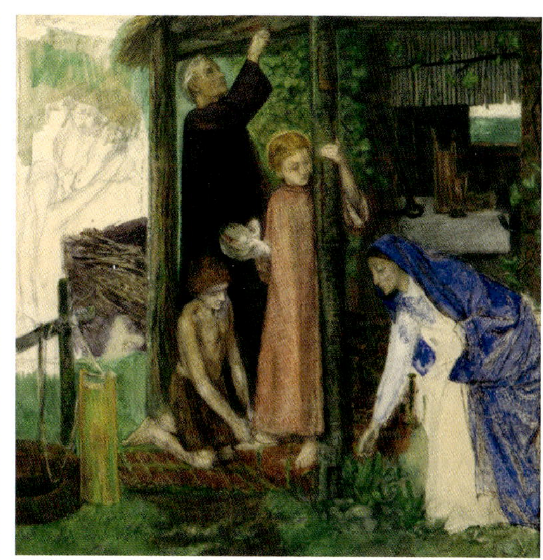

Left: D. G. Rossetti, Dante's Vision of Rachel and Leah, 1855

Right: D. G. Rossetti, Passover in the Holy Family (unfinished), 1855-6

Ruskin offered to relieve her anxieties by buying the drawings, for £30. This generous proposal came with an invitation to tea with the Ruskins. On 11 April, at their suburban villa, a footman answered the door to the young couple, who found the house hung with paintings by Turner. Lizzie was on her best behaviour, speaking little in a modest ladylike manner; Mr Ruskin declared she had the manners of a countess. With great condescension, Mrs Ruskin presented her with powdered ivory, for medicinal use. So Lizzie passed the social test, confirmed the next day when Ruskin drove to Blackfriars to amend the patronage, offering either to buy all Siddal's works as they were produced, or to provide an annual allowance of £150 per year, in exchange for whatever she did produce. She was not at Chatham Place, and when told replied that she preferred to sell work as it was produced. Rossetti favoured the allowance. He was gleeful, according to Brown, and promptly arranged to introduce Lizzie to his family, inviting also the Browns so that it might be less of an interview.

No account of the tea-party on 14 April is known, which suggests it was not a success. Lizzie had previously met William and Christina, but not Mrs Rossetti, nor her elder daughter Maria. The Rossetti women were not unfriendly, but they were devout; perhaps they asked which church Miss Siddal attended, or invited her to their own (Easter was just past). Maybe they simply felt she was not worthy of their beloved Gabriel—or she thought they thought so. There's little doubt that relations began on a reserved if not frosty note. Mrs Rossetti offered to introduce her to their family doctor; with politeness, this was evaded. As it happened, Lizzie was currently in Islington visiting her Aunt Lucy, a grocer's wife. Though Gabriel's family were not snobs, they socialised with the cultured classes, not shopkeepers.

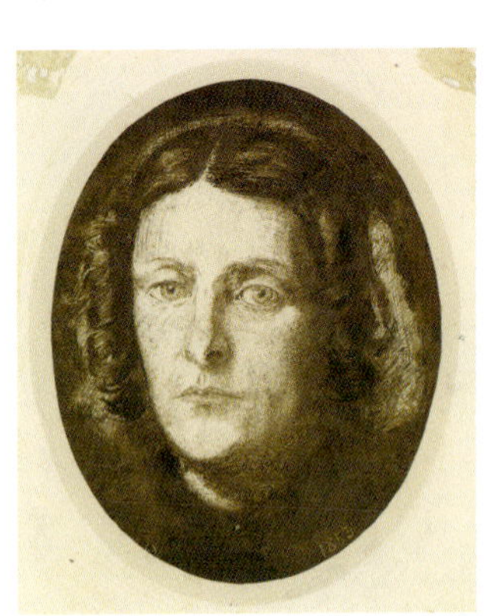

D. G. Rossetti, Portrait of his Mother, Frances Rossetti, 1853

Lizzie, for her part, was not ill-bred, but she was proud and prickly, probably feeling no desire to ingratiate herself with either Rossettis or Ruskins. Gabriel told Brown she would be 'coerced' into accepting the allowance. Ruskin wrote directly, albeit with unpersuasive suggestions. 'I should like you to go to the country immediately,' he declared, adding that Italy would be too exciting, and he would 'plead hard for a little cottage in some sheltered Welsh valley [...] —if possible near a cattle shed —' where she should 'only draw when you can't help it'.[4]

Siddal demurred again, so he wrote again, with equally unpersuasive imagery:

> The plain hard fact is that I think you have genius; that I don't think there is much genius in the world; and I want to keep what there is, in it [...] Utterly irrespective of Rossetti's feelings or my own, I should simply do what I do, if I could, as I should try to save a beautiful tree from being

cut down, or a bit of Gothic cathedral whose strength was failing. If you would be so good as to consider yourself as a piece of wood or Gothic for a few months, I should be grateful to you.

Duly coerced, she accepted the allowance. As some of her existing drawings were already promised to others, she made careful copies of *Pippa Passes* and *Lovers Listening* for her new patron.[5] She was making a sale, not asking for charity.

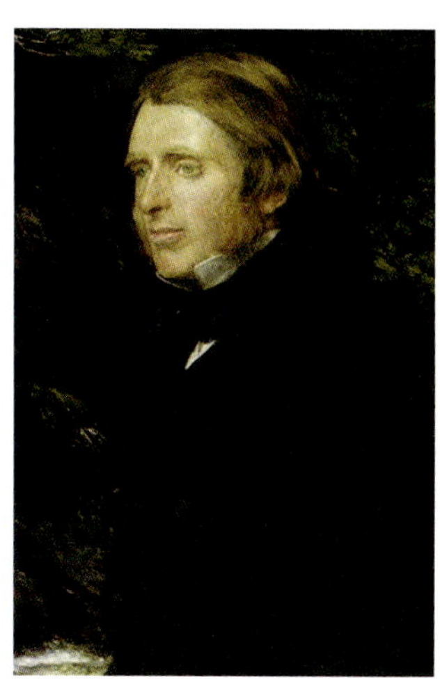

J. E. Millais, detail from Portrait of John Ruskin, 1853–4

Ruskin regarded her reluctance as proof of proud independence. He dubbed her 'Ida' after the heroine in Tennyson's new poem, who sets up a secular college for women and initially declines to marry. Elsewhere he compared her to Flora MacIvor, the passionate heroine of Walter Scott's *Waverley*, who rejects love in favour of the Jacobite cause. Conventionally, as Ruskin would later write, woman's roles within family and state were to heal, redeem, comfort and adorn. Similarly, the recipient of patronage had a duty of gratitude and obedience. Despite limited power, Siddal resisted both.

The allowance was also a tacit means to assist Rossetti, whose motives were surely mixed. A tutor's role was to promote a pupil, get works exhibited, find buyers. A prospective husband's role was to support a future wife. Rossetti was not yet able to do this—and so evaded that pathway, knowing that marital obligations would entail serious production for the picture market.

They all understood this aspect. Ruskin delicately inquired whether Gabriel had 'any plans or wishes regarding Miss S., which you are prevented from carrying out by want of a certain income, and if so what certain income would enable you to carry them out?'[6] He received an ambiguous response, and so wrote more frankly that 'it would be best for you to marry, for the sake of giving Miss Siddal complete protection and care'. Gabriel did not respond to this advice, and by inference it appears both he and Siddal blocked Ruskin's well-meant efforts to plan their lives.

When they met Anna Howitt at this year's RA Summer exhibition, she thought Lizzie looked marvellously well. So much for precarious health. Ruskin continued to advise, telling Siddal she should not design imaginative scenes from old ballads and poems, but concentrate on drawing from observation 'in a dull way from dull things'. This was standard training in draughtsmanship: jars, balls, twigs, leaves. Next, she ought to give up spiritualist séances, which were wildly popular at that moment thanks to the presence of the powerful medium Daniel Douglas Home. Finally, she must leave London; if she would not go to the country she had to visit Ruskin's eminent Oxford friend and professor of medicine, Henry Acland, for a diagnosis.

One senses that to refuse would seem ungratefully ill-mannered. But being Acland's guest meant at least some time with his wife and family (five children including one newborn). Ruskin assured her there were no such social obligations—the visit was a medical consultation. 'You shall be quite independent. You shall see no one,' he wrote, 'you shall have your little room all to yourself.'[7] Nonetheless, female visitors were expected to be sociable.

Acland remembered Siddal as 'a kindly, gentle, quiet person,' which suggests she hardly spoke, adding that he was happy 'to assure Rossetti that his apprehensions concerning her health were greater than her condition called for'. If there were symptoms, they would be due to 'mental power long pent up and lately overtaxed'.[8] This contradictory diagnosis led to the standard Victorian prescription of 'rest' and enforced idleness. The more well-wishers offered remedies, however, the more Siddal refused to identify as invalid.

Siddal's experience of her Oxford visit was not pleasurable. Everyone 'bothered her greatly' and made arrangements on her behalf. The elderly warden of New College showed her manuscripts in the Bodleian library and then 'as a special treat' compared Dürer's large drawing of a black stag beetle with a real one viewed under a microscope. She took tea with the sisters of Dr Pusey, celebrated Tractarian, who was revered by Anglo-Catholics like Maria and Christina Rossetti. And in some way she offended Mrs Acland, to whom Ruskin apologised, excusing Lizzie as 'not ungrateful but sick' and therefore 'headstrong' and 'wilful'.[9] Perhaps she left Oxford without adequate farewells, although she did present Acland with her *We Are Seven* watercolour.

'These geniuses are all alike, little and big,' sighed Ruskin, listing Siddal with Turner, Watts and Millais, 'and I don't know which was or, which is, the wrongheadedst.' They deserved to be whipped, or sent to bed without any bread, as in the nursery rhyme.[10] 'Wilful' was applied to disobedient children. Young women were expected to be submissive, compliant, putting other's wishes before their own. Siddal did not. Her reputation as a 'difficult' woman was growing. And she was very independent in her movements. Ignoring Ruskin's plea for a remote cottage, she went to the then fashionable seaside town of Clevedon in Somerset.

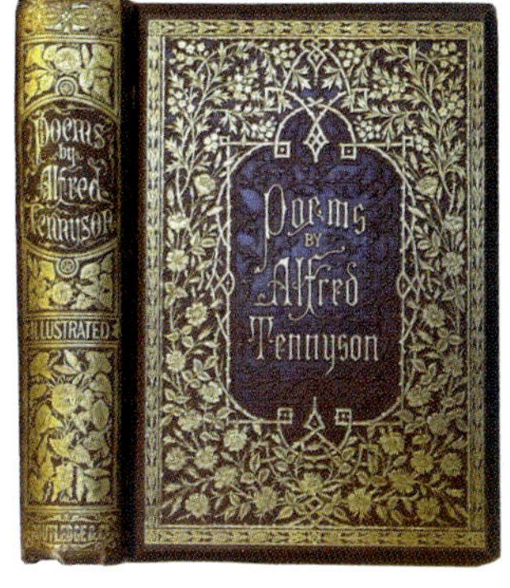

Cover of the second edition of Moxon's Tennyson (1859)

There was a new project underway. The publisher Edward Moxon planned a 'gift book' edition of Tennyson's early (1842) poems, illustrated by leading artists. Commissioning began with an older generation and expanded in 1853 to include Millais, then Hunt and Rossetti. It's possible that knowledge of this prompted Siddal's design for 'The Lady of Shalott', and maybe also the idyllic scene of *Lovers Listening to Music*, if the latter responds to Tennyson's 'Day Dream'. Early in 1855 Moxon spoke to Rossetti, who reported contemptuously of the established artists like Maclise and Mulready. 'The right names,' he told Allingham, 'would have been Millais, Hunt, Madox Brown, [Arthur] Hughes, a certain lady [Siddal] and myself. NO OTHERS'.[11] He also urged his former PRB Thomas Woolner to lobby Tennyson about Siddal's merits. Although in fact the poet had little influence on the choice of illustrators, when Woolner replied that Mrs Tennyson was sympathetic, optimism surged. Siddal began sketching. With energy and invention, she added to her existing Lady of Shalott half a dozen compositions: Morte D'Arthur, showing three Queens with the dying king; Jephthah and his Daughter from the Old Testament via 'A Dream of Fair Women'; St Cecilia from 'The Palace of Art'; and Sir Galahad and Lady Clare from the eponymous poems.

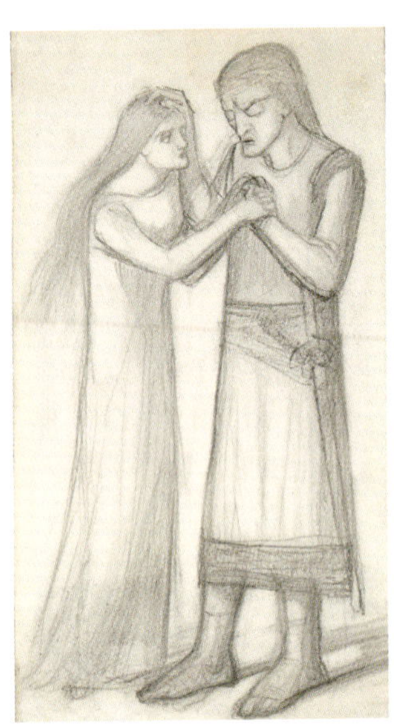

E. E. Siddal, Sketch for Jephthah's Daughter, c. 1855. A biblical heroine, emblem of self-sacrifice for the good of the community

Few of these designs progressed, but the many sketches that Gabriel later collected show visual ideas being worked out and revised. Jephthah's Daughter (from the terrible Biblical tale of a ruler's vow to sacrifice the first creature seen on return from victory) is among the most accomplished, with firmly delineated figures held in a tightly tensed embrace, with tragic expressions. In other sketches the sometimes tentative nature of the lines testifies to artistic study, not casual scribbling. Siddal's designs contributed, moreover, to Rossetti's own final illustrations for Moxon, notably his *St Cecilia* (p. 75) and *Arthur with weeping Queens*. Gabriel was famously dilatory with regard to commissions, and would not deliver for several months.

It would be good to know more clearly how Ruskin's 'allowance' was paid. Siddal will not have had a bank account, and probably relied on Rossetti receiving payment either in cash or a draft drawn on Ruskin's father's bank. Assuming the first quarterly instalment was made around May 1854, how much of the promised annual £150 had Siddal received by the following summer? How much did she need for travel and lodging at Clevedon? Relatively small sums gave a single person great independence. To some extent Ruskin's allowance was regarded as joint income for Lizzie and Gabriel; later in 1855 she was out of funds, having 'lent' him £20.

A woman travelling alone was unusual and indecorous. When Gabriel could not escort Lizzie to Oxford, Ruskin had suggested her sister do so. If no male or relative was available, a servant would suffice. A young lady on her own risked 'insults' in the form of lewd comments, improper invitations, offensive remarks. Siddal appears to have been more intrepid than most.

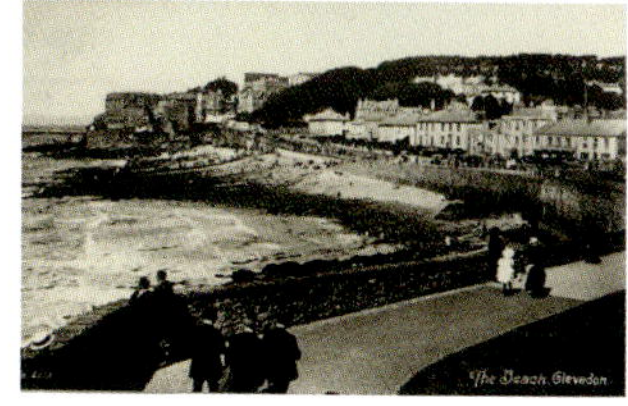

Postcard view of the promenade and beach, Clevedon, Somerset

In a letter to Gabriel, which he relayed to his family, she wrote of wandering on the beach at Clevedon, where a talkative lad of twelve was in charge of the donkey rides:

> The donkey-boy opened a conversation by asking if there was any lions in the parts she comed from. Hearing no, he seemed disappointed, and asked her if she had ever ridden on an elephant there. He had last year when the beastesses was here, and on mounting the elephant for a penny, he felt so joyful that he was obliged to give the man his other two-pence, so he couldn't see the rest of the fair. He wished to know whether boys had to work for a living there, and said that a gentleman had told him that in his country the boys were so wicked that they had to be shut up in large prisons. He never knew hisself no boy what stole anything, but he supposed in that country there was nothing but fruit-trees. He pulled a little blue flower growing out of a rock, and said he liked to let flowers grow in the fields, but he liked to catch one when it grew there and take it away, because it looked like such a poor little thing. He had a project for leading donkeys without

beating, which consisted of holding a grass within an inch of their noses, and inducing them to follow it. Being asked whether that would not be the crueler plan of the two, he said he had noticed that donkeys would always eat even when they were full, so he had only to fill the donkey first. All that could be got in an explanation of why he thought Lizzie some outlandish native was that he was sure that she comed very far, much farther than he could see.

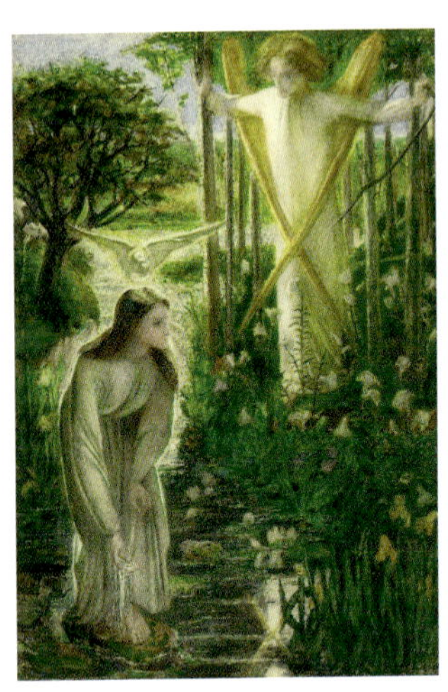

D. G. Rossetti, The Annunciation, 1855

Of the very few surviving letters from Siddal, two contain comical accounts of such encounters. She and Gabriel shared a sense of humour, irreverence towards convention and a taste for spontaneity. When at the end of June Rossetti joined her in Somerset, they made 'longish excursions' in the neighbourhood, including a visit to the clifftop churchyard with the grave of Arthur Hallam, Tennyson's friend mourned in *In Memoriam*. This would have been a touch of literary homage by artists illustrating the Laureate's early poems. Returning to London, the couple carried clumps of wild iris from local ponds, to plant in pots at Chatham Place. The flowers featured prominently in Rossetti's next watercolour, an outdoor *Annunciation* where the Angel appears to the Virgin as she dips her veil into a shallow stream, clustered with pale yellow lilies.[12]

Together they went to Stafford House, London home of the Dukes of Sutherland, open weekly in the summer vacation for well-dressed visitors to view the art collection of Old Masters. Lizzie was extremely well-dressed, as Brown noted: 'Miss Siddal beautifully dressed for about £3, altogether looking like a Queen'.[13] At Blackfriars Brown admired Rossetti's 'wonderful and lovely' studies of 'Guggums' 'one after another, each one a fresh charm each one stamped with immortality'. He was in awe of the delicate draughtsmanship, fine lines and soft hatching that imparts a beautiful frailty to the portraits, and by their quantity

D. G. Rossetti, Elizabeth Siddal, 6 February 1855

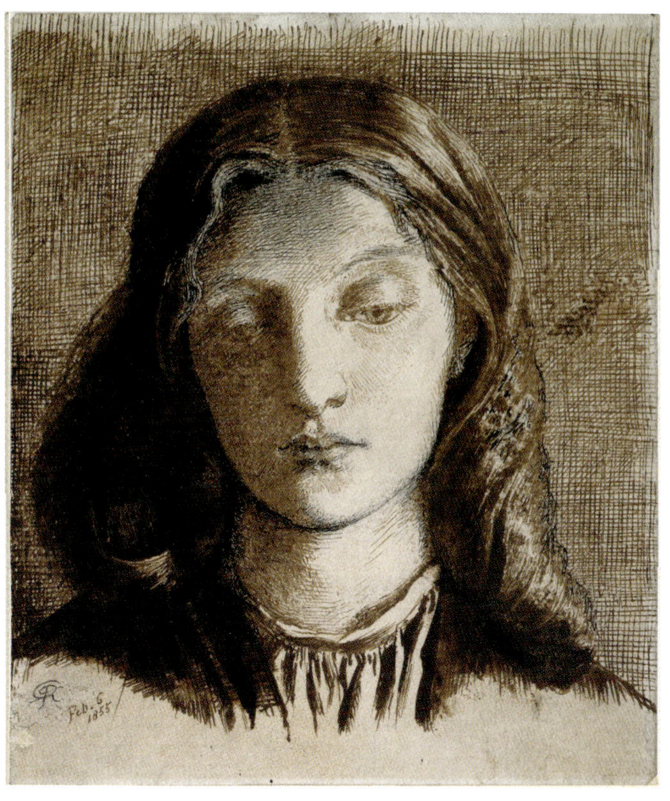

—'a drawerful of "Guggums"; God knows how many [...] it is like a monomania.'[14]

Brown also recorded 'a coldness' between Christina and Gabriel 'because she & Guggum do not agree'.[15] Gabriel was liable to take offence when others did not share his views, and although Christina was too courteous to fall out with Lizzie, the two women were not warm friends. Lizzie no doubt kept her customary distance, while Christina's view of Gabriel's relationship was vividly conveyed in a sonnet that dramatises a visit to an artist's studio, where 'One face looks out from all his canvases'. The poet sees the model in her diverse roles:

> One selfsame figure sits or walks or leans:
> We found her hidden just behind those screens,
> That mirror gave back all her loveliness.
> A queen in opal or in ruby dress,
> A nameless girl in freshest summer-greens,
> A saint, an angel—every canvas means
> The same one meaning, neither more or less.

But also with a clear view of mismatch between fantasy and reality:

> He feeds upon her face by day and night,
> And she with true kind eyes looks back on him,
> Fair as the moon and joyful as the light:
> Not wan with waiting, not with sorrow dim;
> Not as she is, but was when hope shone bright;
> Not as she is, but as she fills his dream.

In August they spent a weekend with the Browns in Finchley. Gabriel slept at a nearby pub, Lizzie in Brown's bedroom and Brown presumably with Emma, young Cathy and baby Oliver. All went for a carriage ride into the country, spending more than Brown could afford, and the following day Lizzie took Emma into London. The two women were the same age and had met their menfolk as models; if Lizzie was the more sophisticated, Emma was a married mother of two, with the social status that carried. They were warm friends. Gabriel followed them and later summoned Brown to join them all at Astley's, a popular circus theatre. But Brown failed to find them. When he reached Chatham Place, Lizzie was in the bed and Gabriel nowhere to be seen.

This was certainly a free-wheeling *vie de Bohème*. On another occasion, Brown recorded, he, Emma and baby Oliver stayed with Gabriel at Chatham Place amid 'all manners and squalls and discomfort'. When Ruskin called the next day, Gabriel ignored the Browns, despite Oliver's yelps from the next room.

With a show of reluctance, Siddal had agreed to spend the winter in the south of France, on Ruskin's recommendation. The chief inducement was a stopover in Paris, the European centre of fashion and art. It was also this year the site of the Exposition Universelle, in emulation of Britain's Great Exhibition; this ran from May to November and the Fine Art section was a principal attraction. The artist Joanna Boyce, some months younger than Siddal, who had two paintings at this year's RA summer show, was already in France for a season of study and had a commission to review the Exposition.

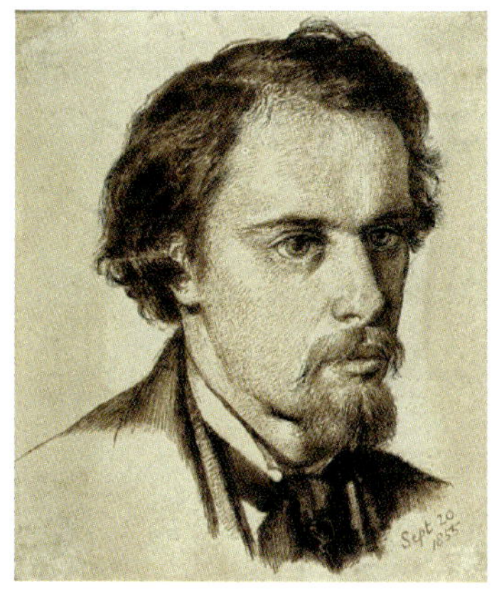

D. G. Rossetti, Self-Portrait, 20 September 1855

But first Siddal had to leave London. On 20 September Gabriel drew a small ink self-portrait, perhaps for her to have while travelling. Solo journeys in Europe being unthinkable, a companion was secured. Named Mrs Kincaid, she is a shadowy figure in the Pre-Raphaelite story, reputedly a relative of the Rossettis but with no such visible link. Of the few Kincaids listed in relevant censuses, only a couple seem eligible: Mrs Elizabeth, merchant's wife in her 30s and Mrs Sophia, in her 60s, with adult daughters Louisa and Mary Ann. As Joanna Boyce noted, one could also advertise for a travelling companion with compatible dates and destination. Possibly the Mrs Kincaid whom Mrs Rossetti and her sons met at a 'farewell party' was found through this means, or word of mouth. She and Siddal sailed for Le Havre on 23 September. Brown lent Gabriel £15 so that he could repay the money he had borrowed from Lizzie.

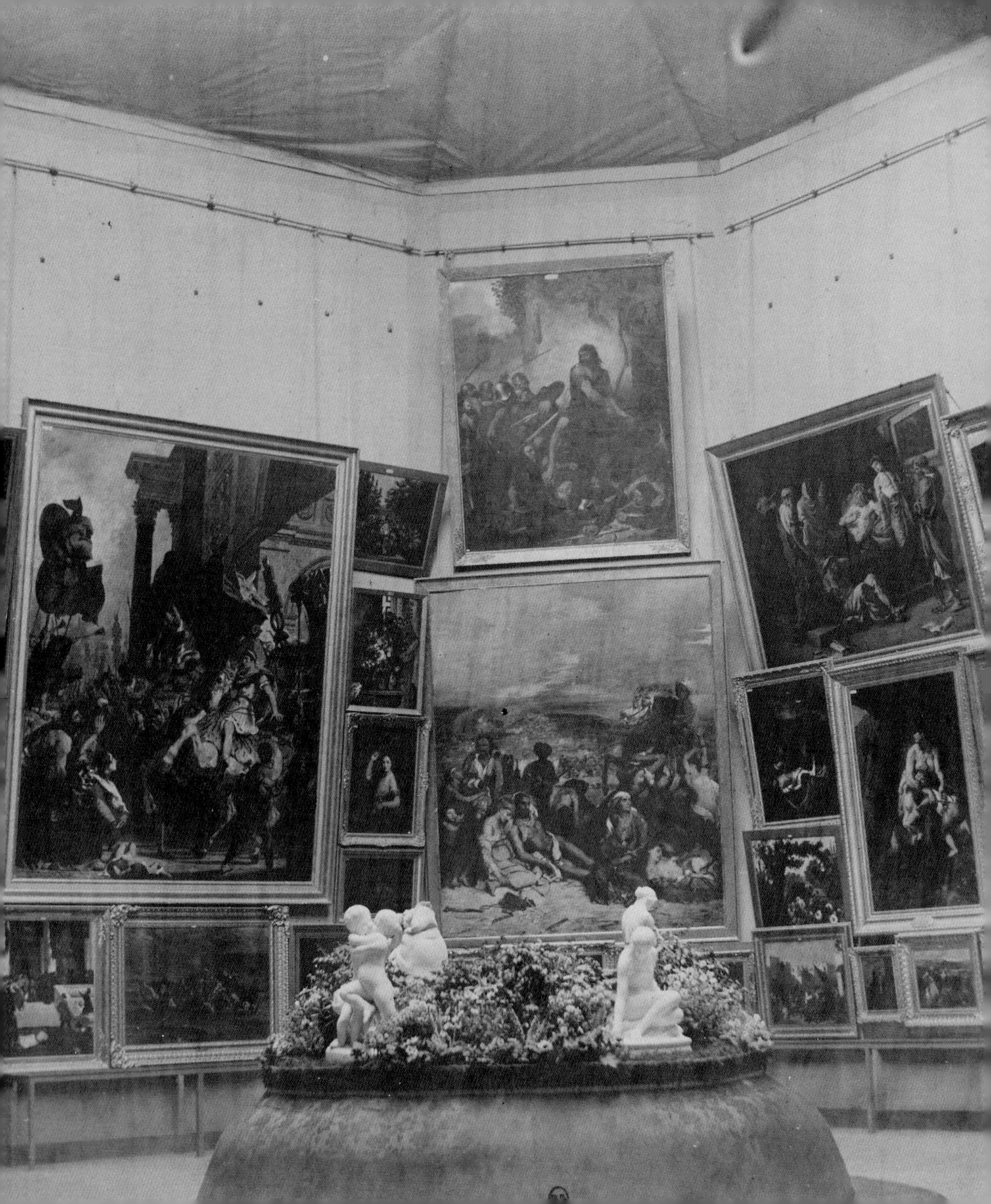

4. FRANCE

Opposite: A.-A.-E. Disdéri, View of Fine Art Section, Exposition Universelle, Paris, 1855. Delacroix's Massacre at Chios, 1824, is visible in the centre

THIS WAS HER first foreign trip. She was travelling as an independent woman, ostensibly for her health, but also as an aspiring artist. Though we don't know how much art history she had learnt from books and engravings—Anna Jameson's *Sacred and Legendary Art* (1848) and *Legends of the Madonna* (1852) are distinct possibilities—this would also be her first sight of the full panoply of contemporary French painting and sculpture. At the Exposition Universelle, so many works were on view, photographs showing pictures hung from high ceilings to dado rail in a typical 19th-century manner, with free-standing marbles and bronzes, that it is hard to judge the effect on a visitor like Siddal with limited knowledge.

British visitors were generally anxious to assess how far their national art fell below French standards. Writing for *The Saturday Review*,[1] Joanna Boyce lamented the absence of work by Paul Delaroche and Ary Scheffer, and awarded pride of place to Thomas Couture and Constant Tryon, with honourable mentions for the history painters Meissonier and Leon Cognier, and vigorous disgust regarding Ingres and François-Joseph Heim. Siddal's opinions are sadly unrecorded. She must also have visited the Louvre, with its unrivalled collection, where she would have seen Leonardo's *Madonna and Child with St Anne,* and the *Fête Champêtre* then attributed to Giorgione.

Few accounts of her life pay attention to her art training and knowledge. Her naïve draughtsmanship and literary subjects seem to preclude all historical study, apart from some interest in manuscript illumination, fostered by Rossetti and Ruskin in their medievalish phase, and apparently reflected in Siddal's small, over-wrought images. By contrast, Boyce continually sought and responded to existing art with critical intelligence. She also always carried a pocket sketchbook, as artists commonly did, for swift or considered rendering of people and places, with constant observation and technical skill. Siddal left no such notebooks, presumably following Rossetti's example and viewpoint that valued imagined designs more than observed ones. At the same time, her experience of studio life and visits to exhibitions indicate that she did attend to other artworks.

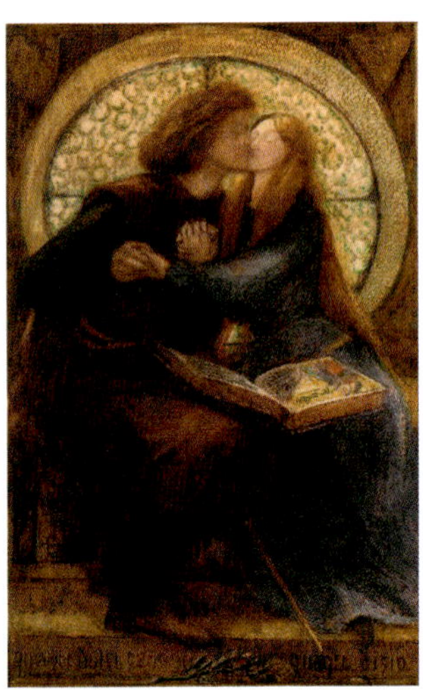

D. G. Rossetti, detail from Paolo and Francesca, 1855

Rossetti offered to take the next instalment of her allowance to Paris. No, replied Ruskin, 'I said I would find funds for you to go into Wales to draw something I wanted. I never said I would pay for you to go to Paris.' In response, Rossetti rapidly produced a lovely, intense watercolour of the Dantean lovers Paolo and Francesca, for which Ruskin paid. Rossetti then travelled to Paris with sculptor Alex Munro for the closing days of the Exposition. 'We enjoyed Paris immensely, in different ways of course,' reported Munro. 'Rossetti was every day with his sweetheart, of whom he is more foolishly fond than I ever saw lover. Great affection is ever so to the mere onlooker, I suppose.'[2]

Of the French painters, Rossetti admired the 'mighty' Delacroix, with religion, history, poetry, romance, drama, still-life and public events of the day. The selection of British art was creditable, including as it did Brown's *Chaucer*, Hunt's *Light of the World*, and Millais's *Ophelia*. One wonders how Siddal felt, seeing her own image amid such company. Gabriel introduced her to Robert Browning, whom he had recently met in London, but sadly Mrs Browning was indisposed. He did not seek out Joanna Boyce, whose brother George was often one of the fellows at Chatham Place; she was now enrolled in a ladies' class at Couture's atelier. Her ambition and independence were equal if not superior to Lizzie's, for unlike Lizzie, Joanna understood and was determined to acquire a full range of painterly skills.

Lizzie was probably equally interested in the Paris fashions. Wide crinoline skirts with a neat bodice and flounced sleeves, in bright silks or tartan weave were in vogue, one magazine noting the richness of fabrics and ribbons, plus 'the quantity and expense of the trimmings, without which a dress cannot be made.'[3]

From England, Ruskin scolded. 'Tell Ida she must go south directly. Paris will kill her or ruin her.'[4] So by the end of November Siddal and Kincaid were en route for the coast of Savoy, between France and Italy, which was still half-independent. The milder climate of the Mediterranean was regarded as healthier than damp, foggy Britain. 'She is sanguine of being able to paint there,' Ruskin wrote at the end of the year.[5] She had her pencils and colours and sketchblock, probably packed into a carrying case with a table-top easel. What was she intending to paint? Probably the Sir Patrick Spens subject and perhaps one of the Virgin and Christ Child scenes—maybe the unrealised Nativity, or the Madonna and Child with Angel. The Louvre may have prompted a response to devotional themes. An out-of-doors version of the Annunciation was begun around this date, and unlocated sketches record a Deposition, with Mary cradling the dead Christ, with St John and the Magdalen, and an Empty Tomb, where two Marys meet an Angel. All were standard episodes in the Life of the Virgin.

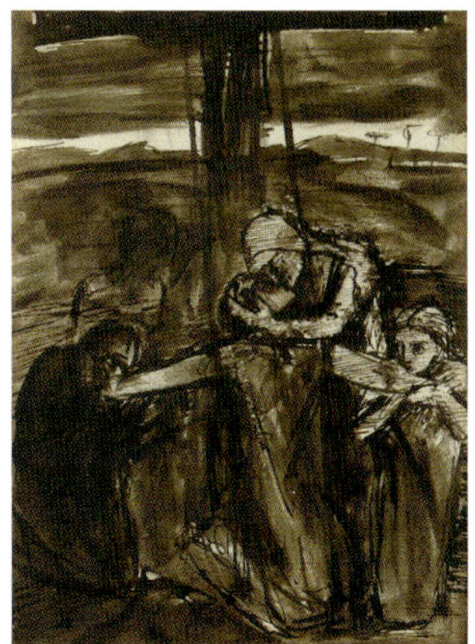

E. E. Siddal, Sketch for Descent from the Cross, c. 1855

Next to nothing is recorded of her time on the Riviera, where the destination was Menton, which before the building of the corniche road was reached by boat. According to one guide, the journey from Paris to Mentone—still retaining its Italian pronunciation—took several days, with stopovers at Lyons, Valence, Toulon and Nice. The whole trip from London cost about £20.[6] In Menton she lodged at the Hôtel des Princes, from where Siddal wrote with traveller's ennui:

> There was an English dinner here on Christmas Day, ending with plum-pudding, which was really very good indeed, and an honour to the country. I dined up in my

> room, where I have dined for the last three weeks on account of bores. First class, one can get to the end of the world but one can never be alone or left at rest'.[7]

She and her travel companion seem to have parted company, though it is possible that Mrs Kincaid also spent the whole season on the Riviera. A livelier and indeed vividly descriptive letter sent after Christmas about collecting money from the central post office in Nice, conveys the daunting experience of foreign bureaucracy. Visitors were obliged to lodge their passport with the local police, and to present it when receiving a registered packet:

> On your leaving the boat, your passport is taken from you to the Police Station, and there taken charge of till you leave Nice. If a letter is sent to you containing money, the letter is detained at the Post Office, and another written to you by the postmaster ordering you to present yourself and passport for his inspection. You have then to go to the Police Station and beg the loan of your passport for half-an-hour, and are again looked upon as a felon of the first order before passport is returned to you. Looking very much like a transport, you make your way to the Post Office, and there present yourself before a grating, which makes the man behind it look like an overdone mutton-chop sticking to a gridiron. On asking for a letter containing money, Mutton-chop sees at once that you are a murderer, and makes up its mind not to let you off alive; and, treating you as Cain and Alice Gray in one, demands your passport. After glaring at this and your face (which has by this time become scarlet, and is taken at once as a token of guilt), a book is pushed through the bars of gridiron, and you are expected to sign your death-warrant by

writing something which does not answer to the writing on the passport. Meanwhile Mutton-chop has been looking as much like doom as overdone mutton can look, and fizzing in French, not one word of which is understood by Alice Gray. But now comes the reward of merit. Mutton sees at once that no two people living and at large could write so badly as the writing on the passport and that in the book; so takes me for Alice, but gives me the money, and wonders whether I shall be let off from hard labour the next time I am taken, on account of my thinness. When you enter Police Station to return the passport, you are glared at through wooden bars with marked surprise at not returning in company of two cocked-hats, and your fainting look is put down to your having been found out in something. They are forced, however, to content themselves by expecting to have a job in a day or so. This is really what one has to put up with, and it is not at all comic when one is ill. I will write again when boil is better, or tell you about lodgings if we are able to get any.[8]

As with the Clevedon donkey-boy, this confirms Siddal's taste for humorous anecdotes, worked up for effect. Referencing two notorious evildoers—Cain and the fraudster Alice Gray—it spins a shaggy story from an everyday incident. The letter also reveals that Siddal was suffering from boils, but able to travel to Nice from Menton and back again.

Was she really seeking solitude by dining alone, or was the world-weary tone a mask for low feelings in what was then a fairly isolated place and where she did not speak the language? A small town where lemons and olives were the main products, in winter Menton's population of about five thousand grew by some three hundred invalid tourists. Coincidentally donkey

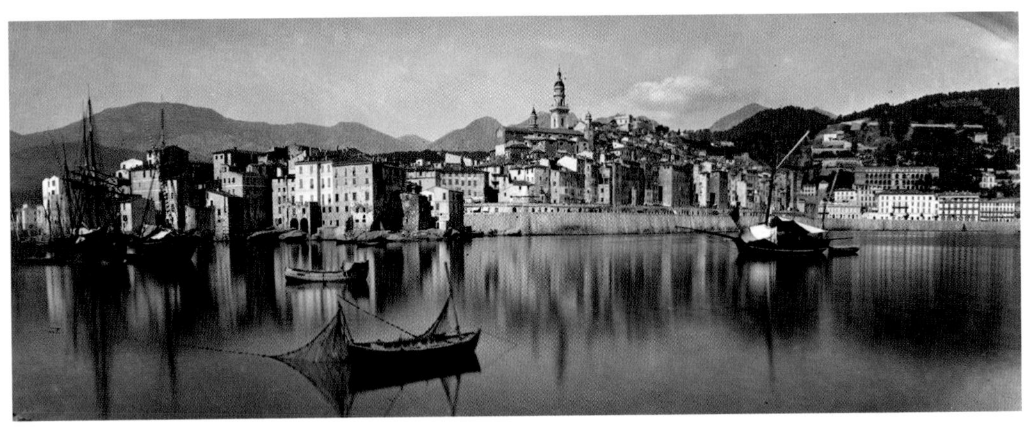

Menton towards the end of the 19th century

rides were a chief attraction, second only to the sunshine. There were few amusements, although these were expanding to cater for the northern visitors. Lizzie was accustomed to bustle and anonymity in London; the encounter with postal and passport officials could have been a welcome diversion.

There was, however, a daily *passeggiata* along the Promenade du Midi before lunchtime. 'Let us take a walk,' wrote a travel writer:

> The fishing operations of the morning are over, and the boats engaged in it have been drawn up upon the beach. The water carts, small wooden boxes drawn by men, have performed their rounds, and the roadway is moist, but is rapidly drying up under the burning beams of the hot sun; but the dust is laid. The sea is tranquil—not a ripple disturbs it, except at the very edge, where it lazily turns over in the tiniest of waves, as if the exertion implied far too much fatigue for this melting day. A ship has ventured out of the harbour, spreading its white sails in vain attempt to catch a breeze. A flock of gulls are resting, in quiet happiness and contemplation, their snowy bosoms on the glassy

water. In the distance, bright Bordighera is stretching its long green sleeve far into the blue sea, its fair hand lighted by the sun; while its cathedral window, like a jewel on the finger, catches and glistens with a blazing ray.[9]

And then, in February, came Carnival, a weekend of 'complete holiday' when 'every one turned into the streets, or took possession of windows, balconies, and other salient points; while the promenade was ornamented with long Venetian decorated poles' and balconies draped with flags. The inhabitants put on cloaks and masks and peppered everyone with confetti pellets. A procession of costumed men on foot and horseback, carts with giant papier-mâché figures, ladies in carriages, and musicians, was followed on the final evening with fireworks and a huge effigy set ablaze.

One hopes Siddal enjoyed the masquerade spectacle. Looking back, the previous twelve months had been good, thanks to Ruskin's generous patronage. She had met her prospective in-laws, visited Oxford, Clevedon and Paris and now Menton, as an independent traveller. Looking forward to 1856, although the commissions to illustrate ballads and Tennyson had not happened, she had repurposed these plans, so with Ruskin's support had excellent chances of success. *Sir Patrick Spens* was complete, and the illustration to Tennyson's 'Lady Clare' well advanced. With good fortune, Rossetti would also achieve financial stability and they would marry, perhaps by the time she was 30.

Or, was life less promising? Was she lonely and listless, half-sick and at risk among a crowd of invalids suffering from infectious lung diseases, with a faraway sweetheart who was surely having a better time?

If he was, he preferred to represent himself in melancholy terms. In London, around the date of Menton's Carnival,

Gabriel composed morose Valentine lines to his 'dear dove divine', who was not there to keep the clock wound and his own self presentable:

> Some time over the fire he sat,
> So lonely that he missed his cat;
> Then wildly rushed to dine on tick—
> Nine minutes swearing for his stick,
> And thirteen minutes for his hat.
> And now another day is gone [...]
> Come back, dear Liz, and, looking wise
> In that arm-chair which suits your size,
> Through some fresh drawing scrape a hole.
> Your Valentine and Orson's soul
> Is sad for those two friendly eyes.

In an old romance not to be confused with any saints, Valentine and Orson were twin brothers separated at birth; Orson grows up in savagery, Valentine in courtly circles; reunited, they become knightly champions. If Gabriel was unkempt Orson, he was also (now blending this with the early Christian patron of lovers) Lizzie's disconsolate Valentine.

Yet his affairs were starting to prosper. He had drawn several medievalish watercolours for Ruskin, who complained of their technical faults, and had influenced Ruskin's analysis of Gothic art for the third volume of *Modern Painters*. Other compositions included Dante's dream of Beatrice's death, a monk illuminating a manuscript, Lancelot and Guinevere embracing over the effigy of King Arthur. At Ruskin's request, he took a weekly evening class at the new Working Men's College, finding pleasure in teaching skilled woodworkers and decorators how to draw. His apartment was a mess, with painting equipment all over the table, sketches and books strewn on the floor.

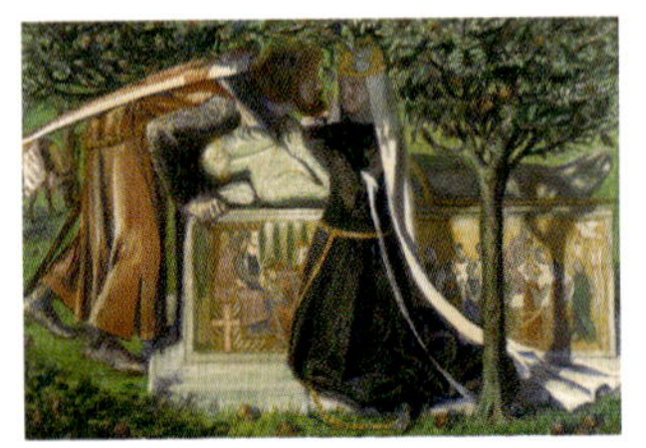

D. G. Rossetti, Lancelot and Guinevere at King Arthur's Tomb, 1855

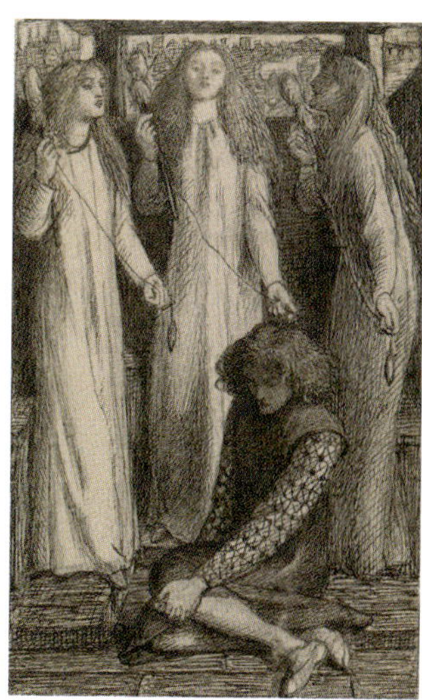

D. G. Rossetti, Maids of Elfen-Mere, 1854

Holman Hunt was back from Palestine with a number of highly original subjects, including a Dead Sea scapegoat, and expecting that his former model Annie Miller had in his absence and at his expense acquired the manners and education needed to become his wife. A group of young University men were producing a magazine, which described Rossetti's drawing of the *Maids of Elfenmere* as 'the most beautiful illustration ever seen' and asked rhetorically why the author of 'The Blessed Damozel' did not publish anything new. This was very gratifying. So too was his meeting with one of the young men, Edward Jones (later self-dignified as Burne-Jones), who aspired to be an artist but had no formal training. Most gratifying of all, the architect J. P. Seddon persuaded the diocese of Llandaff in south Wales to commission a triptych altarpiece for their cathedral. On 4 March the local MP Henry Bruce came to talk themes and fees.

This was Rossetti's first big commission, which he would 'go into with a howl of delight after all my small work', he told Allingham. If he wrote to Siddal with the good news, the letter has not survived; if, as is probable, she kept it, it was destroyed with all others after her death.

Possibly she had moved to Nice, because when she wrote to acknowledge receipt of her quarterly allowance, without enthusiasm for the sun-bleached scenery, Ruskin replied: 'I hate Nice myself.' In recommending the Riviera, he added, he had not known where she would like; instead she ought to try the Alps, where were red-roofed bell-towers, green and white torrents, deep green pines, white snows and 'blue valley distance'.[10] To Rossetti he suggested that she had spent too much. Siddal headed home. Gabriel thought of going to meet her in Paris, but did not—she seems to have now been a confident solo traveller, which Rossetti was not. So when she arrived back in London around the end of April 1856, the omens were good.

The Crimean War had ended, the troops were returning, to general celebrations. The Royal Academy summer show contained Millais's hastily reconfigured family group *Peace Concluded*, Henry Wallis's *Chatterton*, Joanna Boyce's portrait of her severe hostess in Paris and, most controversially, Hunt's *Scapegoat*, whose symbolism puzzled many. William Rossetti was now sedately engaged to Henrietta, daughter of the editor of *The Spectator*, for which he wrote. Rumour claimed that both brothers were to marry—'D. G. to a young lady, an artist. You will guess who,' wrote Fred Stephens.[11] It was a reasonable assumption, especially once the £400 Llandaff commission was secured. Millais, who was preparing to marry Effie in Scotland and had broken with Rossetti over his continuing friendship with Ruskin, came to mend fences. Urging matrimony on all his fellows, and praising work in progress, he 'kept bursting into raptures as only Millais can,' observed Brown.[12]

Presumably using the latest tranche of her allowance, Siddal rented rooms of her own in Weymouth Street, in elegant Marylebone. She went to visit the Browns, now living in Kentish Town. The next day Emma, who was again pregnant, was taken to Weymouth Street. Finding Lizzie had left the Browns', Gabriel followed, accusing Emma of inciting Lizzie's discontent, which she did not, Brown indignantly observed, 'for poor Miss Sid complains enough of his goings on not to require that sort of thing'.[13] This was the first in a series of small rows and reconciliations that marked this summer, all recorded in Madox Brown's diary.

Victorian women were supposed to be docile rather than combative. The role of wives and girlfriends was to support and soothe, not to argue. And if Lizzie was demanding, one must also recognise that Gabriel was equally 'difficult'—wilful, capricious,

E. E. Siddal, The Ladies' Lament from the ballad of Sir Patrick Spens, 1856

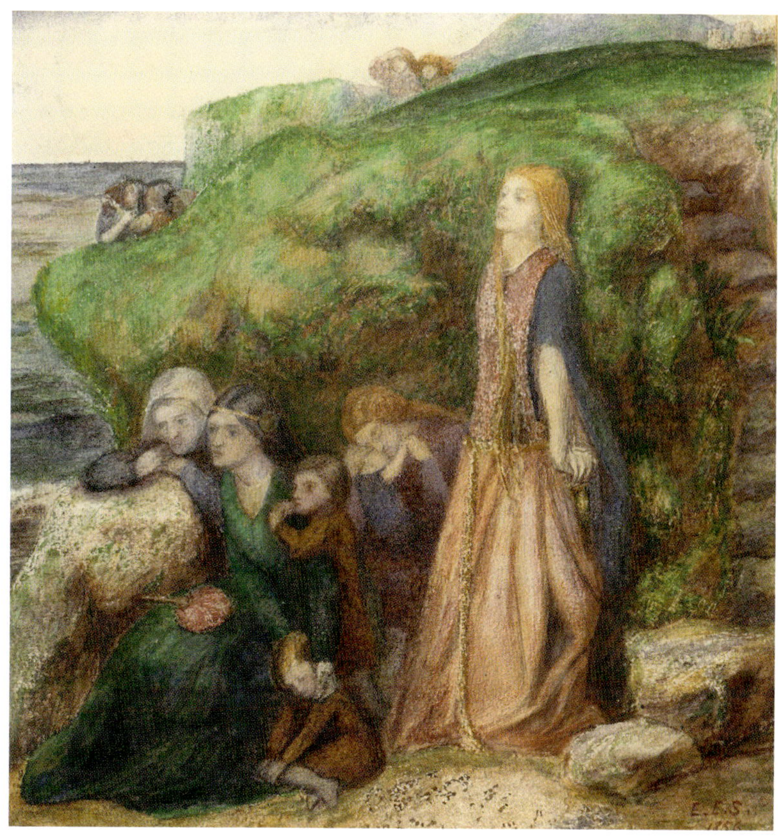

moody, often downright unpleasant. He could be an expansive, generous host and friend, but equally a sour, irascible back-biter. Not surprisingly, she fought back.

But to focus first on her work. In July Brown noted that Siddal was busy painting. The watercolour *Sir Patrick Spens* was finished, neatly signed 'E.E.S 1856'. So too was a very small picture of two figures in woodland that acquired as title *The Haunted Tree*. It shows a blue-gowned female shrinking away

E. E. Siddal, The Annunciation, 1856. Also known from its inception as The Haunted Wood, this shows the Archangel appearing to the Virgin Mary with hands raised in benediction

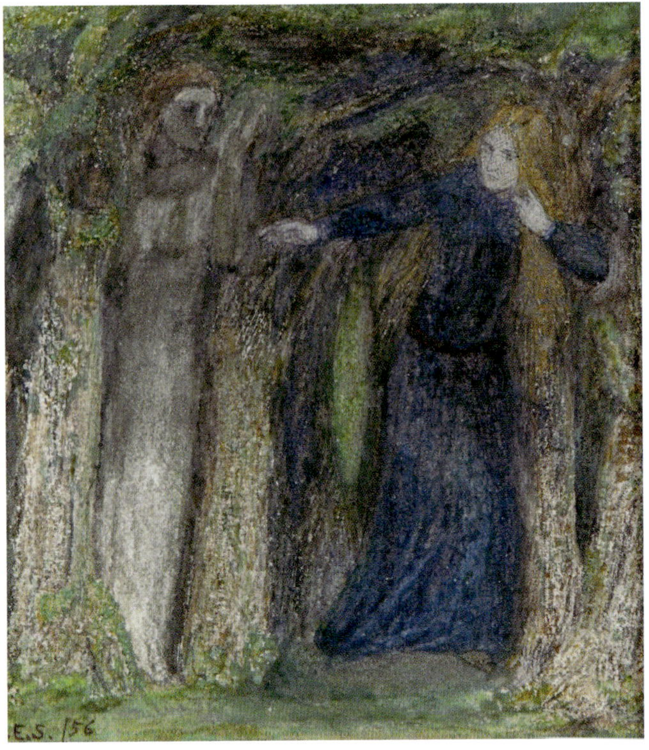

from a white-gowned figure with upraised hands. Although taken as a ghostly encounter, a compositional sketch shows this was in fact a version of the Annunciation featuring the Virgin Mary and Archangel Gabriel, whose gesture represents his words 'Be not afraid, for you have found favour with God.' The drawing is unusual in placing this traditional scene in a forest setting. It joins Siddal's other images of Mary, showing her in the stable with a newborn baby; by a window with the Christ Child standing on her lap; and encountering an angel at His empty tomb. Rossetti's own Life of the Virgin sequence, that began with his first exhibited work, *The Girlhood of Mary*, includes the comparable outdoor *Annunciation* (see p. 56), which shows Mary standing in a sunlit stream, with the archangel hovering between trees, arms outstretched. Most likely, Siddal had worked on one or more of her own Marian watercolours while in Menton. Ruskin invited her to see his collection of missals—illuminated prayerbooks—and take the air in his suburban garden.

Her next subjects were watercolour versions of the Tennysonian subjects, 'St Agnes' Eve' (not confused with Keats's text) and 'Lady Clare', a dialogue about class and marriage. When Clare's lowly parentage is revealed, she proudly disdains to conceal it. 'I am a beggar born' she tells her noble suitor, who marries her nonetheless. The scene Siddal chose is that where Clare's real mother begs her not to disclose:

> 'Nay now, my child,' said Alice the nurse,
> 'But keep the secret all ye can.'
> She said, 'Not so: but I will know
> If there be any faith in man.'

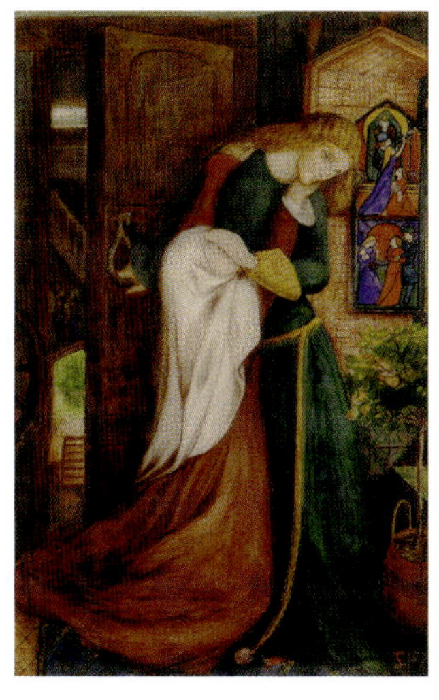

E. E. Siddal, Lady Clare, 1857. Illustrating Tennyson's ballad about social class

The intricate compositional study for this, presumably designed for potential wood-block printing, shows Alice kneeling with raised arms to implore Clare, who turns resolutely away, one hand covering Alice's face. In the watercolour version, Alice wears a red robe and white wimple and Lady Clare a green gown with gold girdle. To the right a window embrasure has stained glass depicted the Judgment of Solomon, typologically echoing the 'true mother' theme. The image reflects the manner of Ruskin's 15th-century missals, and that of the chivalric scenes Rossetti would soon be composing in response to William Morris's Froissartian poems. Morris and Ned Jones were Gabriel's new best friends, but Siddal did not meet them. She was less often at Chatham Place.

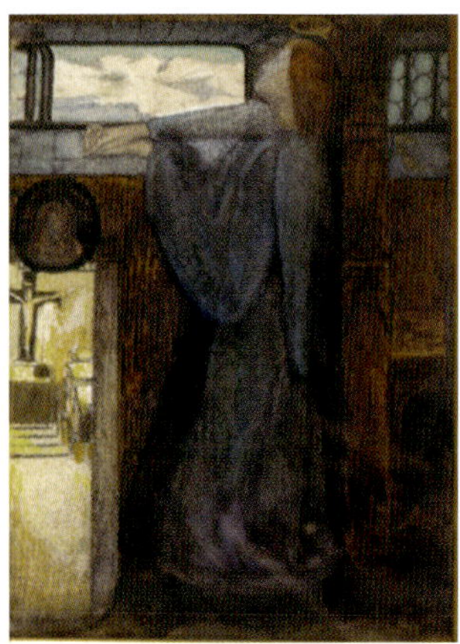

E. E. Siddal, St Agnes' Eve, 1854

Like several of Siddal's artworks, *Lady Clare* portrays embracing figures in moments of intense emotion. Simpler but with a solo figure, *St Agnes' Eve* depicts the nun of Tennyson's poem in a high room, yearning for her Heavenly Bridegroom while gazing over a frozen landscape, with a view into a chapel:

> Deep on the convent-roof the snows
> Are sparkling to the moon:
> My breath to heaven like vapour goes;
> May my soul follow soon!
> The shadows of the convent-towers
> Slant down the snowy sward …

A third work in this sequence is *St Cecilia*, also illustrating Tennyson but never worked up in watercolour. Compositional studies show a woman swooning while playing a portable organ, the bellows being worked by a kneeling angel; a window opens behind. For his own belated illustration to the poem, which he drew this summer, Rossetti 'borrowed' the design, according to William,[14] moving the scene to harbour ramparts and bringing saint and angel close together. One can't infer that Siddal was annoyed with this appropriation; she may have regarded it as part of their collaboration.

She was, however, annoyed with other behaviour, notably his new friendship with Annie Miller, the model who during Hunt's absence had been learning the manners fit for his wife. Emma Brown had received a comparable education before her marriage, while according to the Ruskins, Siddal was already ladylike, despite modelling. But Hunt was in no hurry, while Annie wanted commitment. In Siddal's absence, Rossetti had employed her as a model in his jewelled picture of *Dante's Vision of Beatrice's Death*. He then took her to dine at Bertolini's and to Cremorne Pleasure Gardens, where she danced with

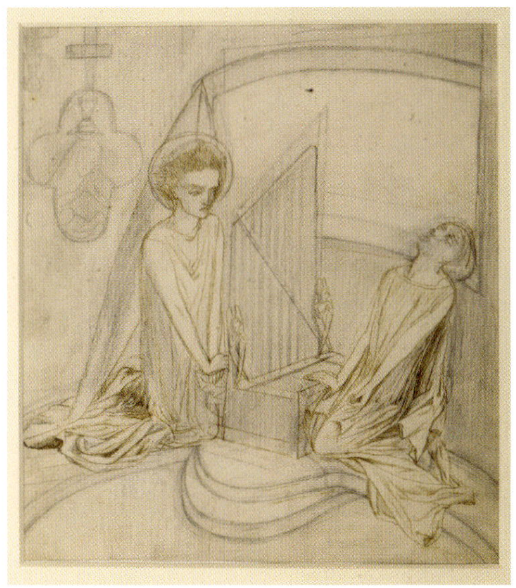

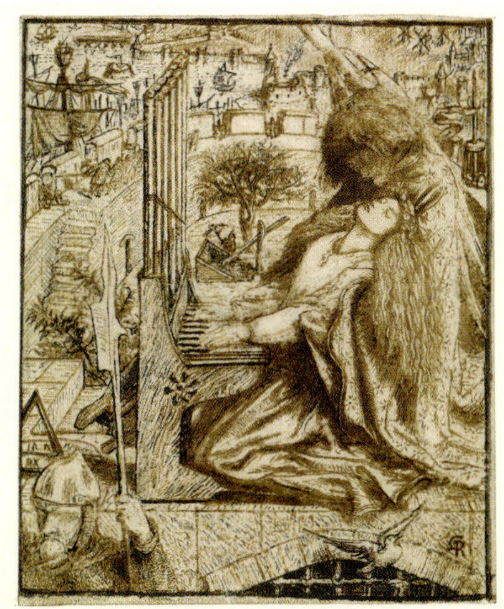

Left: E. E. Siddal, Sketch for St Cecilia, c.1855

Right: D. G. Rossetti, St Cecilia, 1856-7

George Boyce. William Rossetti took her out on the river. Hunt poured out his 'perplexities' to Brown, who commented that 'they all seem mad about Annie Miller'. Lizzie, who had been enjoying herself with theatre visits, a splendid Indian cloak and a seaside trip to Ramsgate with Emma, now learnt of these flirtations. Both she and Hunt blamed Gabriel, who later blamed Hunt.

But then all blew over; Lizzie and Gabriel were again 'on the best of terms' and invited to be godparents to the Browns' new baby Arthur, born on 16 September. Moreover, Rossetti told Brown late one evening, he intended to marry at once, and was just waiting for the 'tin' or money from sale of a painting—probably *Dante's Dream*, sold to Ruskin's friend Ellen Heaton—and 'then off to Algeria!!' on honeymoon. Brown was surprised by the announcement and no doubt sceptical, because,

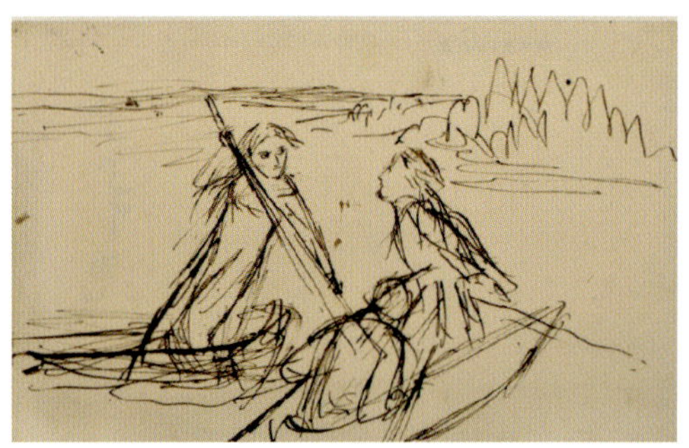
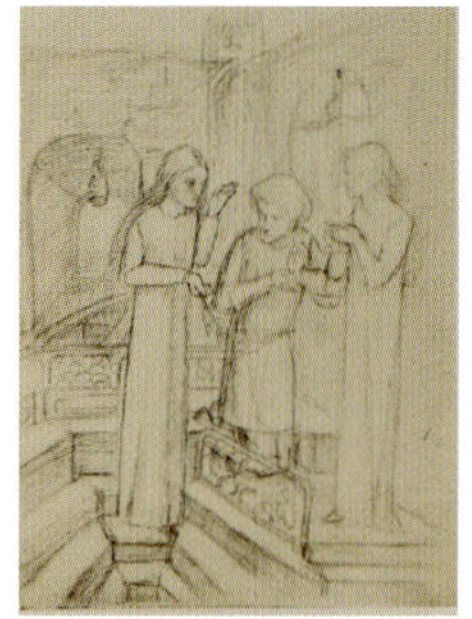
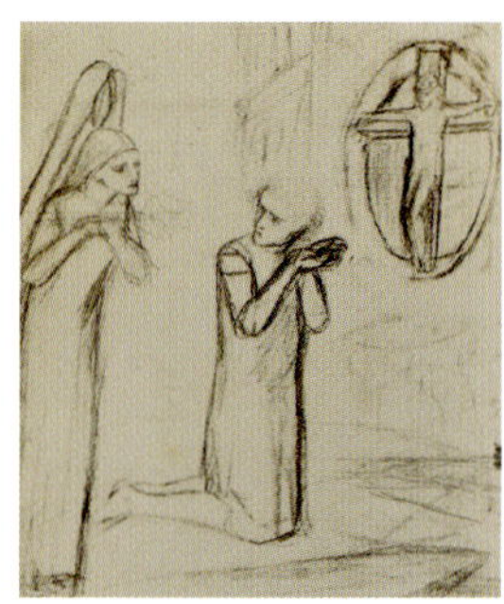

E. E. Siddal, compositional sketches, 1855. Left: figures in lightweight skiffs. Right: two studies for the Ruined Chapel, illustrating Tennyson's poem 'Sir Galahad'

as Lizzie reported later, when the money arrived Gabriel 'told her all he was going to do with it but never a word about marriage'. In fact, his prospects were buoyant: in addition to the Llandaff commission, he had money from several new patrons for the Dantean subjects. Whether angry or flaunting her independence, Lizzie went instead with her sister to Bath, which was still a fashionable spa town. She stayed through October, November, December.

Having finally delivered his woodblocks to Moxon, Rossetti joined her in Bath, where it rained. Together, they worked on a watercolour illustration to Tennyson's poem of 'Sir Galahad and the Holy Grail'. The somewhat gnomic text is a monologue by Galahad extolling chastity, where the wandering narrative includes a 'secret shrine', a 'magic bark' and three angels bearing the Grail. Sketches by Siddal show Galahad in a ruined chapel, with two flying angels; Galahad kneeling in a sort of skiff; Galahad kneeling before a crucifix; and Galahad kneeling on an altar between two standing figures. The finished composition depicts him in the skiff with folded oars floating through a flooded chapel, where angels hover holding chalice and patten. The angels have Siddal's features, Galahad has Rossetti's. To the left is a high ox-eye window above a lower

E. E. Siddal with D. G. Rossetti, Sir Galahad, c.1855. This has both artists' initials, probably added when Rossetti completed the drawing by adding colour washes. Composition and outlines are by Siddal

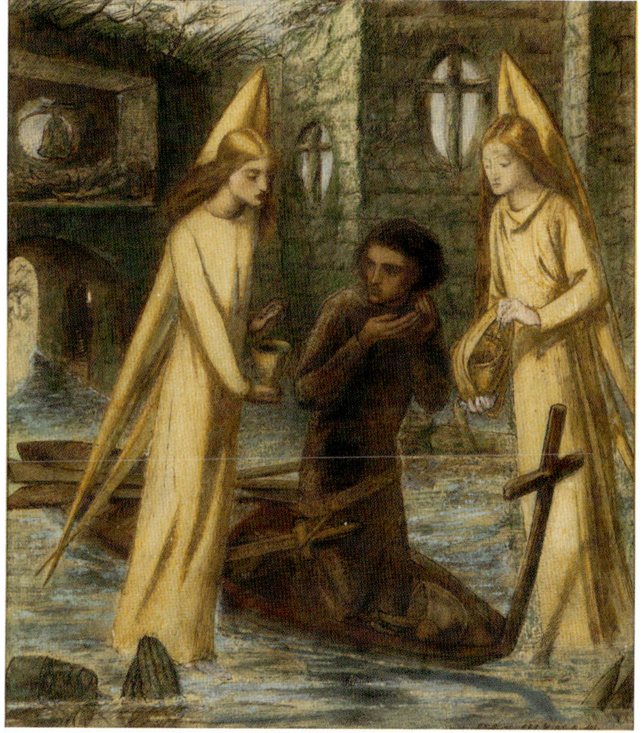

door—by this date a signature motif in her pictures. With the quirky detail Rossetti loved to insert in drawings, the helmet and clasped hands of a stone effigy poke up through the flood. The piece is executed in virtual grisaille, with a blue wash on the water. It is signed 'EES inv EES & DGR del', which means she designed the composition and they executed it together; this is the clearest evidence of artistic collaboration to date. It was presented to Ruskin.

5.
DEBUT

HOW SHOULD WE INTERPRET the many versions of Siddal's biography that emphasise ill-health and emotional dependency? Historians in post-antibiotic ages who read extensively in Victorian correspondence can regard it as an era of acute hypochondria, when physical danger was discerned in a rain shower, night time air, geology or damp bed linen. Real risks, from contaminated water, polluted atmospheres, unhygienic surgery and bacterial infection, were only gradually being recognised. Another misconception held that those in lower social classes were more robust than gentlemen and ladies: ironically, poor health was thus seen as a marker of status. When belied by longevity, this was ascribed to the intense care invalids took to avoid sickness.

Naturally, there were many dangerous, contagious diseases and conditions aggravated by noxious air, water, septic surroundings and unrefrigerated food. Levels of illness were undoubtedly high, with few curative methods beyond the body's own capacity to overcome pathogens. Walter Deverell had died of kidney failure; Tom Seddon died of dysentery in Egypt that autumn; Maria Rossetti had chronic erysipelas, a streptococcal skin condition. No-one was immune and anxiety was lifelong. It is, however, notable that at this period, Siddal was able to travel as extensively as anyone. The insistence on Siddal's frail health by those without medical knowledge—Wilkinson, Barbara Smith, Mrs Ruskin—must be set beside evidence of her active life of journeys and visits, and Acland's failure to find any physical impairment. The oft-repeated diagnosis of lifelong ill health was resisted by Siddal herself—unless it chimed with her wishes.

What of emotional frailty, and the narratives that describe her as living with Rossetti throughout the 1850s, vainly wishing for marriage? As far as facts are available, they indicate that during their twenties both artists pursued largely independent lives in the same manner as other engaged couples from the middle classes. Long engagements were based on the view that weddings be postponed until husbandly earnings could maintain a household, which meant covering the costs of rent, furnishings, clothing, food, fuel, servants' wages, medical expenses, sons' schooling, travel and, if necessary, support for infirm and unwaged relatives. Delaying marriage was prudent. It also offered more social freedom. Although engaged women were bound by rules of decorum, in marriage, women had housekeeping responsibilities, maternal health risks and possible subservience to a domestic bully. These constraints were balanced against the legal security whereby a husband was obliged to keep a wife. This obligation began with an engagement, a formal promise of marriage. Once obtained, women often waited years until finances allowed.

Although less conventional than other couples, Siddal and Rossetti lived within this framework. Millais might sing its praises and the Browns urge their friends on, but few voices commended marriage without assured income. Neither Lizzie nor Gabriel wished for long-term reliance on Ruskin, and, had they calculated, their living costs were probably less separately than together. On the other hand, perhaps Siddal did wish to marry sooner rather than later, and her departures from London, to Clevedon, Ramsgate, Bath and elsewhere were designed so that she be missed. She had as yet only private promises. We can only observe her actions, not read her thoughts.

Everyone knew Gabriel Rossetti was wayward, moody, 'so dogmatic and so irritable when opposed', as Millais commented; ready 'on the most trivial occasion to hate and backbite anyone' according to Brown.[1] Not long before,[2] Christina Rossetti had composed a monologue that she never published, but which 'embarrassed' William when he did so, and which in driving triplets surely dramatises her brother's inconstancy:

> I wish we once were wedded—then I must be true [...]
>
> Listen, Eva I repent, indeed I do my love [...]
>
> Can I bear to think upon you strong to break not bend,
> Pale with inner intense passion silent to the end,
> Bear to leave you, bear to grieve you, O my dove my friend?
>
> Why do you face me with those eyes so calm they drive me mad,
> Too proud to droop before me and own that you are sad?
> Why have you a lofty angel made me mean and cursed and bad?

Gabriel described his moods as the 'blue devils' and lamented his dislike of doing even what he himself had chosen. 'As soon as a thing is imposed on me as an obligation,' he wrote, 'my aptitude for doing it is gone; what I ought to do is just what I can't do.'[3] Now, instead of painting, he preferred poetry, prompted by requests to publish old pieces in an American magazine edited by Ruskin's friend William Stillman, and more immediately in *The Oxford & Cambridge Magazine* issued by his new university friends. They also introduced him to Malory's version of the Arthurian legends, declaring it much greater than Tennyson's.

On her return from Bath, Siddal took new lodgings, in Eland House halfway up the hill to Hampstead village,[4] with a direct track across fields to the Browns' house. It has been too easily assumed that in today's terminology she and Gabriel 'lived together', before marriage; in fact, she had found her own rooms in a large house serviced by a housekeeper. She was also in regular contact with her family in Southwark.

In the new year of 1857, more collaboration was proposed. Exact details are unclear, but it appears that Hunt and Brown revived an old Pre-Raphaelite idea of an artists' 'college', with adjacent studios and apartments for married couples. They hoped to initiate the plan, inviting also Rossetti, who confirmed that he would be married by the time this came about, and then Ned Jones, who since mid-summer had been engaged to young Georgiana Macdonald.

To discuss plans further, at the end of February, Brown walked over to Eland House, where he found Lizzie and Gabriel with Mrs Siddall, who was visiting her daughter. This is a key detail, as it is easy to overlook Lizzie's relationship with her family. Brown explained the scheme and left, only to hear from Gabriel the following morning:

> My dear Brown, when you first spoke on Tuesday evening of two married couples as beginning the scheme, I thought you meant Lizzy and me for the second; and on finding you did not, I refrained from saying anything, simply because Lizzy has sometimes lately shown so much displeasure on my mentioning our engagement (which I hoped was attributable to illness) that I could not tell how far her mother was aware of it, or how Lizzy would take my mentioning it before her.[5]

What is to be made of this statement? It is a thousand pities that neither Lizzie's nor her mother's account of the event is recorded, because Gabriel's cannot be trusted. Why doubt that Mrs Siddall knew of the engagement? Or that Lizzie would wish it to be mentioned? If Lizzie disliked it being mentioned, was this in terms of angry sarcasm? More likely, Gabriel preferred his promise to marry was not witnessed. Marriage being a legal commitment, to renege could lead to jilted partners suing for breach of promise.

When she and Gabriel were alone, Lizzie voiced her

objections to the scheme, saying 'that she understood only a range of studios, and would strongly object to living where Hunt was, of which objection of hers I had no idea to any such extent'.[6] This was surely disingenuous, after Gabriel's flirtations with Annie Miller, the future Mrs Hunt. He claimed that his participation in the scheme wholly depended on Lizzie, who was now 'quite embittered and estranged from me on this account'. As a result, no more was heard of collective living. More was heard of marriage, however, although always ambiguously.

Please would the Browns not speak to Lizzie about the proposed scheme? 'Kind and patient she has been with me many and many times, more than I have deserved,' he wrote. 'I trust this trouble is over.' He spoke again to Brown about getting married, even borrowing £10 for the licence to permit weddings without weekly banns being read in church. But then the money went elsewhere; altogether Brown was owed £42 by Gabriel and 'Miss Sid'.[7]

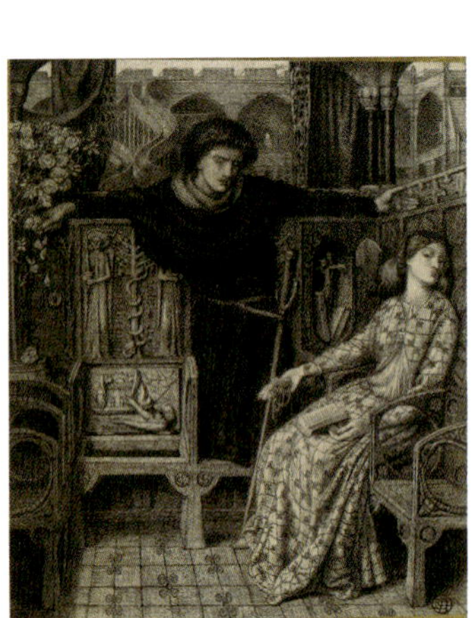

D. G. Rossetti, Hamlet and Ophelia, 1857–8. In this scene, Hamlet is 'ramping about and talking wildly' as Ophelia aims to return his gifts

Evidently, now Rossetti had laid this obligation on himself, he resisted; 'what I ought to do is just what I can't do.' One can't know what Siddal felt. One might infer she chiefly wished their engagement be more publicly known. She would not have been reassured by one of Gabriel's new drawings, illustrating the scene from Shakespeare where Ophelia returns Hamlet's betrothal gifts, and he replies: 'No, not I. I never gave you aught'. Then:

> 'I did love you once'.
> 'Indeed, my lord, you made me believe so.'
> 'You should not have believed me [...] I loved you not.'
> 'I was the more deceived.'
> 'Get thee to a nunnery.'

The tone of this exchange is very like Rossetti's peevish meanness when in a bad mood.

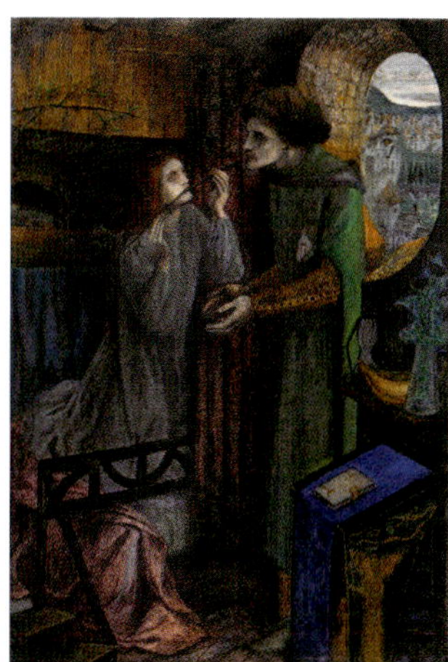

E. E. Siddal, Clerk Saunders, 1857. Exhibited at the Pre-Raphaelite show, Russell Place, and in the USA

Siddal resumed work on her illustration for the ballad of Clerk Saunders and May Margaret, first designed three years before, now working the composition in colours. It is, incidentally, an image of steadfast love—love unto and beyond death. As in Keats' 'Isabella', Margaret is a gentlewoman, Saunders a lowly clerk, whom her brothers conspire to murder. Saunders' spirit then appears to Margaret, asking she reaffirm her love. She does so, sealing her fate, which is to follow him into the grave. Siddal's design, set in Margaret's bedchamber, shows her lover's ghost materialising through the wall as she kisses a branch to plight her troth. In the woodblock version, he appears in his shroud; in the watercolour he wears a long medieval scholar's gown, in emerald green. Once again, the figures have Siddal's and Rossetti's features. The picture is signed and dated 'E. E. S 1857'. Again, unlike Rossetti's elaborate monogram signature, Siddal simply used her initials.

Eclipsing this year's Royal Academy, a vast exhibition of 'Art Treasures' opened in Manchester on 7 May 1857, drawing visitors from home and abroad. Its chief aim was to display Old Master works from Italy and Flanders, giving British viewers an overview of European art history, together with ample selections of British art down the ages, even including 'modern'—that is, contemporary—pictures, by Millais and Hunt.

Madox Brown was prompted in response to organise a 'Pre-Raphaelite' show in London, roping in the Rossetti brothers and securing loans from a score of fellow artists. As at the RA, most works were for sale. Oils, watercolours and line drawings were mixed together. Mounted in rooms at 4 Russell Place, off Fitzroy Square, this untitled show opened on 25 May with 72 artworks, rather hastily assembled. Brown's ten works included *The Last of England*, a portrait of William Rossetti and a tender study of baby Arthur, aged three days. One attraction was the opportunity to see pictures by Gabriel, who had not shown publicly since 1852. He and Brown wished to invite Joanna Boyce, who this season had one small painting hung at the RA, and another more dramatic piece rejected. It was 'a crime against justice' declared her future husband; the selectors ought to have given especial care to a young woman of such genius.[8] After a swift visit to the Manchester show, Boyce left London on a long European trip, and so could not participate at Russell Place. Here Rossetti exhibited his Moxon illustrations, having earlier sent Joanna photographic copies. Thus it turned out that Siddal was the only female exhibitor.

Joanna Boyce's personal position can usefully be compared with Siddal's. Currently she was struggling to reconcile her artistic ambitions with the demands of her insistent suitor Henry Wells, a dilemma compounded by the fact that her widowed mother's quarrelsome behaviour made Joanna unable to live at home. Although her siblings were supportive, the lack of a settled base affected her career, so marriage offered advantages. But she knew the downsides. Agreeing to her engagement to Wells, she told him firmly she was 'really determined not to marry for four or five years—I want you to know this now, that you may if you like run off with the ring.'[9] This situation puts the on/off Siddal-Rossetti relationship in perspective. Wells wanted the security of a wife to take care of domestic matters. Siddal needed the security of commitment, but like Boyce recognised the benefits of independence. (However, it needs noting that Boyce's long-desired professional visit to Rome was possible only in the company of an art school friend with an Italian husband; and that before the trip was over she had recognised Henry's value and married him.)

To the Russell Place show, Siddal contributed six works, Rossetti eight, Arthur Hughes six, Millais five and Holman

Hunt four. For Siddal, it was an exhibition début, admittedly at a minor venue, but in good company and certainly more prestigious than the usual places available to women artists, typically known for decorative flower pieces and amateur works.

All but one of Siddal's exhibits were described in the small catalogue as 'sketches'. Even the watercolour *Clerk Saunders* was 'Sketch for a Picture', as was *We Are Seven*, presumably borrowed back from the Aclands. The other items comprised the line drawings *Pippa Passes* and *The Lady of Shalott*, the small oil *Self-Portrait* from 1853-4 and the watercolour *Annunciation*, here entitled *The Haunted Tree*. As argued above, this certainly represents an Annunciation, and I cannot easily explain its Haunted Tree title. Just possibly, this was a jokey appellation, such as artists often give to images ('it looks like a phantom' etc.). Just possibly, the serious title was withheld because Rossetti's outdoor *Annunciation* was also exhibited. Although this appeared untitled in the catalogue, when it came to printing the exhibit list two such atypical Annunciations were perhaps deemed unwise. It is, however, intriguing that both works appeared in the same exhibition. Lizzie's address, for potential patrons, was listed as 'Miss E. E. Siddal, Eland House, Hampstead', Gabriel's as '14 Chatham Place, Blackfriars Bridge'.

Ruskin cut short his visit to Russell Place, on seeing Millais's portrait of Effie with a garland of foxgloves, and then attacked Millais's new works at the RA, writing that it was 'not merely a loss of power' but a catastrophic 'reversal of principle'. *The Athenæum* welcomed Rossetti's 'mystic' designs, but warned that watercolour sketches did not have the value of large oils.[10]

In *The Saturday Review,* the poet Coventry Patmore made a special, if brief assessment of Siddal's work. Her drawings displayed 'an admiring adoption of all the most startling peculiarities of Mr. Rossetti's style,' he wrote, 'but they have nevertheless qualities which entitle them to high praise'. The self-portrait was 'promising', *Pippa Passes* and *We Are Seven* deserved attention. Though highly praised by some, *Clerk Saunders* 'did not please us so much'.[11]

Shortly before this notice appeared, Patmore and his wife had met Ruskin's admirer Charles Eliot Norton, of Boston, who was on an extended visit to Europe with his family. On 27 June they had been pleased by the Russell Place exhibition, as Norton informed his mother:

> Many of the pictures are interesting, some of them beautiful, many of them full of thought, and as careful, exact copies of nature, some of them can hardly be surpassed. Rossetti's are by far the best, for in force and beauty of colour he stands above the others, and also in depth and delicacy of imaginative power. Among his pictures are those of 'Mary the Mother of Jesus' and the 'Mary Magdalene' that we saw at Ruskin's last year, the picture of Dante's vision at the time of the death of Beatrice and, as a companion piece to this, the anniversary of the death of Beatrice, representing Dante becoming aware of the presence of persons who had been watching him as he drew an angel upon certain tablets.[12]

Though Norton's letter home did not mention Siddal, he praised it verbally. 'Many thanks for what you so kindly say of Miss Siddal's drawing,' Rossetti wrote to Norton on 22 July. 'I am sure it will give her additional pleasure to hear it. She begged me to thank you from her.'[13] Norton purchased as well as praised, commissioning two subjects from Rossetti and buying *Clerk Saunders*, for 40 guineas. Which must have been very pleasing to Siddal, and a vindication of Ruskin's generous allowance, which she now relinquished.

Ruskin was in Manchester, where he lectured on the 'political economy of art', urging his audiences to patronise living artists and invest in Old Masters rather than in fabrics and fripperies for the latest fashions:

> There was much complaining talk in Parliament last week, of the vast sum the nation has given for the best Paul Veronese in Venice—14,000£. I wonder what the nation meanwhile has given for its ball-dresses! Suppose we could see the London milliners' bills, simply for unnecessary breadths of slip and flounce, from April to July; I wonder if 14,000£ would cover them.

Such trimmings were as ephemeral as snow,

> but the Paul Veronese will last for centuries, if we take care of it; and yet we grumble at the price given for the painting.[14]

On his return home, Ruskin was surprised by Siddal's decision, and embarrassed by his delayed response. He wrote:

> Dear Rossetti,—I don't know when I have been more vexed at being out of town, as I have been since Saturday; as Ida's mind and yours must have been somewhat ill at ease thinking I was vexed, or something of that kind. I shall rejoice in Ida's success with her picture, as I shall in every opportunity of being useful either to you or her. The only feeling I have about the matter is of some shame at having allowed the arrangement between us to end as it did, and the chief pleasure I could have about it now would be her simply accepting it as she would have accepted a glass of water when she was thirsty, and never thinking of it any more.

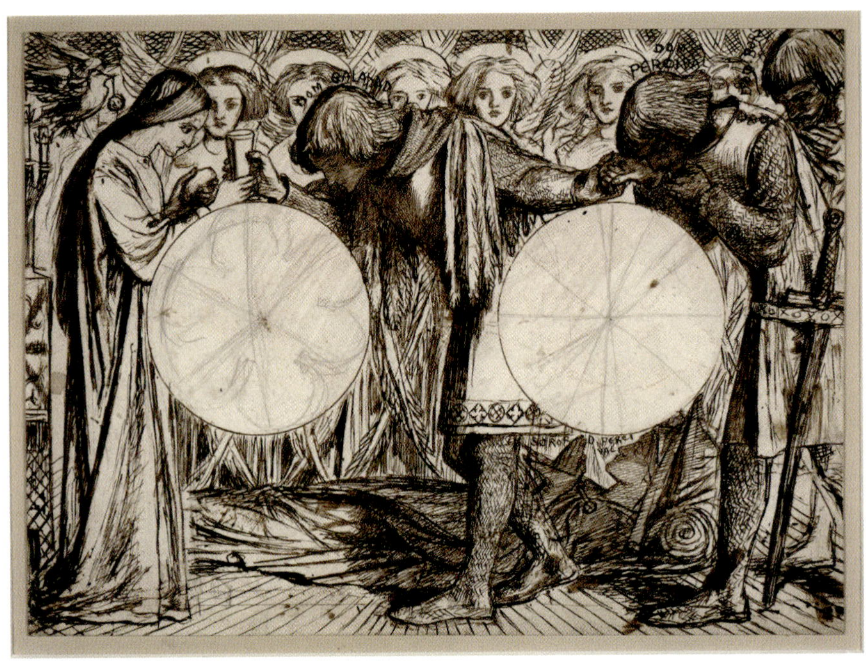

D. G. Rossetti, Study for the Quest of the Holy Grail mural painting for Oxford University debating chamber, 1857. The large circles indicate the high windows that the compositions were obliged to accommodate

Inviting Gabriel, Lizzie and Maria Rossetti to lunch, he wrote:

> Just do as you and your sister and she feel it pleasant or find it convenient [...] if I don't see you or hear from you I shall expect you to dinner at two if it be fine [...] If it would be more convenient to you to put it off for a week, do, or even till full strawberry time.[15]

It isn't clear what Ruskin meant about the subsidy ending 'as it did', unless he had inadvertently allowed payments to lapse. Thanks to the Nortons, Siddal was currently in funds, probably retaining the Hampstead lodgings until Michaelmas. Rossetti, meanwhile, had suddenly decamped to Oxford, to take part in a new collaborative scheme with his new young colleagues. 'What

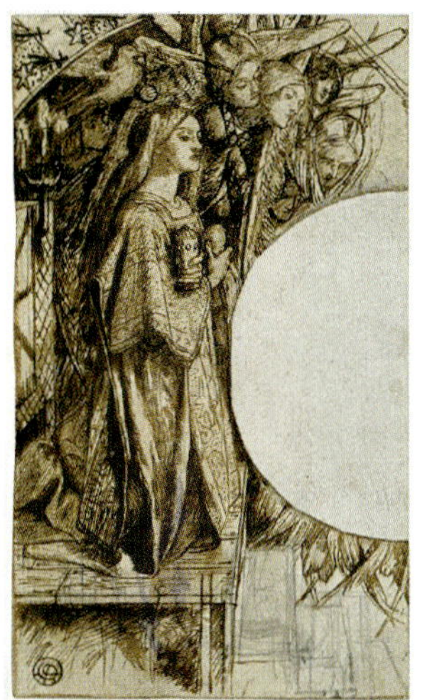

D. G. Rossetti, Study for the Angel Holding the Holy Grail, 1857

do you think I and two friends of mine are doing here?' he wrote to Barbara Smith in early August. 'Painting pictures nine feet high with life-size figures, on the walls of the Union Society's new building. The work goes very fast and is the finest fun possible.'[16] The friends were Morris and Jones, soon joined by Arthur Hughes and Spencer Stanhope. The building was a debating chamber for the University Union, where patrician students developed their speech-making skills. The murals depicted scenes from the *Morte Darthur*, featuring knights of the Round Table. Stanhope chose Sir Gawain, Morris Sir Tristram and Rossetti selected Sir Lancelot. Using Malory's text, in place of Galahad's attainment of the Holy Grail, he showed Lancelot's failure, his vision blocked by the image of Guinevere.

Through the late summer, the fellows had such a great time. 'It is really very jolly work in itself, but really one is mad to do such things,' Rossetti told Brown, who was mourning the sudden death of baby Arthur. Morris, who had money, commissioned a helmet and chainmail from a blacksmith. Curious visitors came to watch, including 'a new poet who is charming'—a ginger-haired lad named Algernon Swinburne. 'We began with enthusiasm and repented, if we repented, afterwards,' recalled Ned Jones; 'when Gabriel willed a thing it had to be done [...] I thought—this man could lead armies and destroy empires if he liked; how good it is to be with him.'[17] Seeking female models, Ned and Gabriel recruited a dark-haired servant girl named Jane Burden.

6.
SHEFFIELD

SIDDAL WAS NOT INVITED to Oxford, so she went to Sheffield. Cause and effect are not proved: she was an experienced traveller; Sheffield was her father's hometown, so she had relatives to visit. A later informant recalled her mother meeting both Lizzie and Clara Siddall in the city, which suggests that the trip coincided with Clara's summer holiday from her job at a garment wholesaler.[1] Lizzie stayed for about twelve weeks, while Clara returned home. We know virtually nothing about their paternal family, and of the 80 male Siddalls listed as cutlers living in Sheffield in the 1861 Census, none appears a likely grandfather. Only William, born 1814, and George, born 1804, seem possible uncles. But we may assume an extensive cousinage, for altogether 165 Siddalls were living there that year. Lizzie could have gone in some glory, not quite as a daughter made good, but as someone who knew the up-and-coming artists of what the press called 'the three-lettered race', because although the PRB had disbanded in 1853, many were still talking of it, and she had exhibited with the Brethren. Moreover, *Clerk Saunders* now travelled to North America, to feature with 180 other pictures in the 'American Exhibition of British Art' that visited Boston and New York this winter.[2] She was, too, a friend of the well-known John Ruskin, now turning from art to political-economic affairs.

In later years, research added to the context. The local Congregational Church year book for 1857 recorded that Miss E. E. Siddall was a member of the Queen Street Chapel in Sheffield. The Congregationalists were old-established Dissenters, dating from Cromwellian times, popular with the independent craftsmen of Sheffield. Her father was a member, so if Lizzie lodged with relatives, she will naturally have attended their chapel, a square red-brick building designed for sermon and choral singing. To be registered there indicates some active membership.

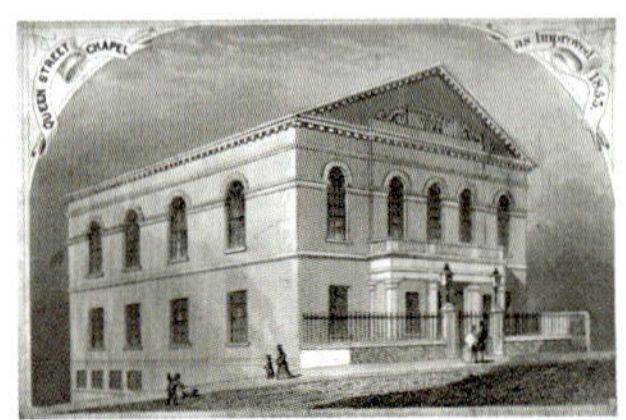

Congregational Chapel, Queen Street, Sheffield, showing the improvements made in 1853

William Ibbitt (after), South-East View of Sheffield, 1855

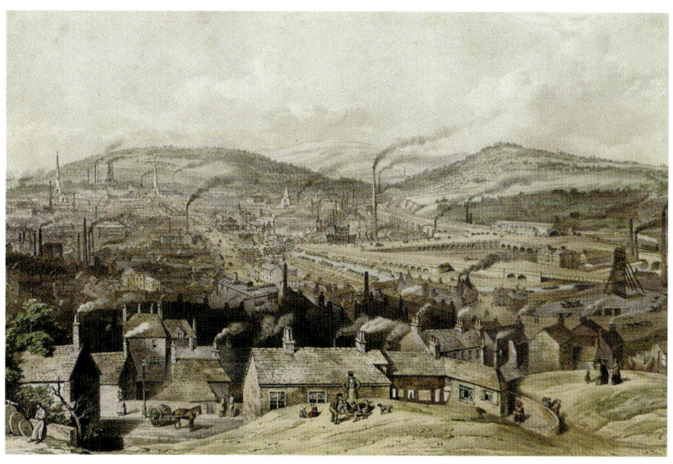

Further details emerged later. One informant claimed that his neighbour had a sketchbook that had belonged to William Ibbitt, silversmith, topographical artist and Radical councillor, which contained a portrait sketch of Miss Siddall. Another stated that Ibbitt had brought Lizzie to meet the informant's parents, who were unfortunately not at home. An Isabella Gilchrist offered her mother's memory of meeting the Siddall sisters at Ibbitt's house.[3]

It was Ibbitt who wrote Siddal's only obituary. In it he described how she had 'taken a house on Eccleshall Road' and visited local sights; but strangely he did not mention her connection with the School of Art. Later investigation revealed that this was in fact where she met her main contacts in Sheffield. Two correspondents to the local newspaper in 1911 confirmed they had been fellow students. One, identifying herself as 'A. S.', stated that Miss Siddall attended the School regularly and joined the student excursion to the Manchester 'Art Treasures'. The sculptor-craftsman Charles Green, who supported Ruskin's endeavours in the city and was just a few years younger than Siddal, also recalled the Manchester trip, adding that the school's policy was to welcome visiting artists to the studios. The testimony of A. S. and Charles Green may be relied on (unlike that of William Rossetti who told an unnamed correspondent it was 'improbable' that Lizzie had ever studied at Sheffield, or anywhere else).[4]

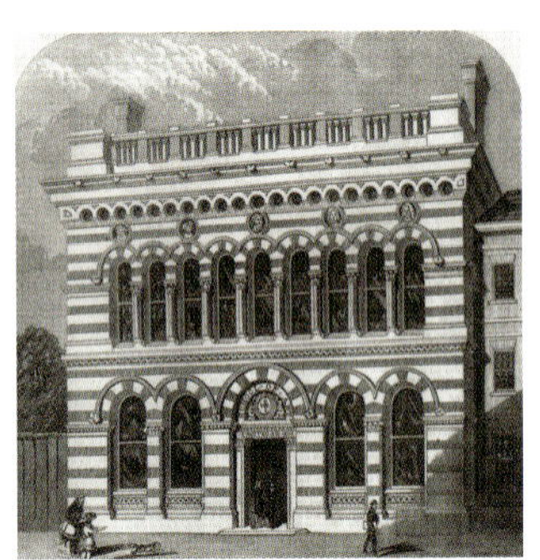

Sheffield School of Art, 1856

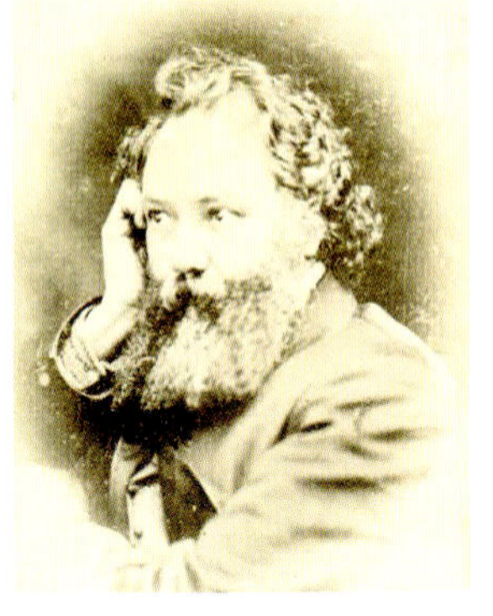

Photograph portrait of Young Mitchell, director of the Sheffield School of Art

It's notable that what began as a summer visit to relatives soon became a working holiday, spent in an art environment. As it's also hard to verify much in the jumble of mainly hearsay information, let's return to what we can know. The Sheffield School of Art was one of the network of Government Schools of Design established and funded by the Board of Trade 'for the improvement of ornamental art'. The first, originally located in Somerset House, was the one directed by Walter Deverell's father. Rossetti's friend William Bell Scott was director of the Newcastle School from its founding in 1844. The Sheffield School's principal from 1846 to 1865 was Young Mitchell, who presided over its first triumph in 1851 when students won four gold medals for applied design at the Great Exhibition, and also over its move to purpose-built premises in the city centre in 1857. Mitchell had studied under Ingres in Paris; a self-portrait endows him with dark, Byronic features. By the time of a later photograph, he had a full Victorian artist's beard.

The art school thus had a high reputation, attracting both artisans and middle-class students, who typically enrolled by the term and the class. They were expected to profit from example and instruction, rather than through grades or exams; incentives came from externally awarded prizes. Most of the male students were in manufacturing or apprenticeships from the age of 14, so attended evening classes, while daytime classes were for women and fee-paying men. When not in a class, students were

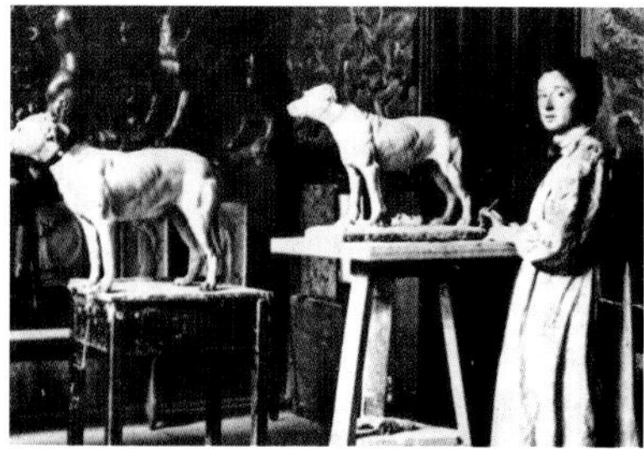

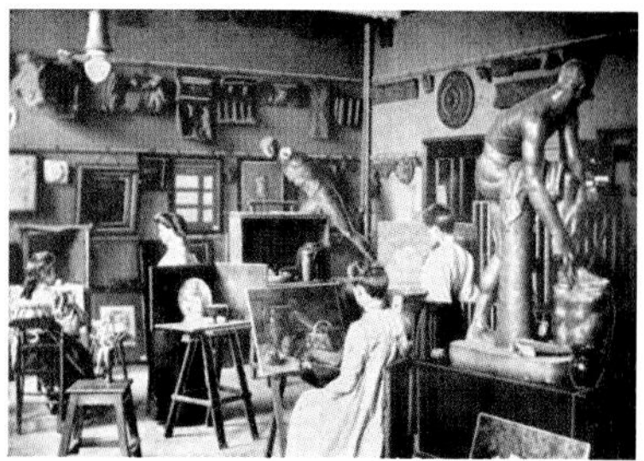

Later view of students in the cast room, Sheffield School of Art and Design, c. 1905-17

permitted access to the studios, to work on drawings and designs, a facility extended to others on payment of a monthly fee.

A. S. remembered that Siddal 'worked in the Figure Room' and 'remained after class hours':

> So did I, and as I ate my luncheon and wandered through the rooms, I met with her and we talked sometimes, or if Mr Young Mitchell, our headmaster, joined us, I listened to them and it was then that I first heard of Ruskin and the Pre-Raphaelites.[5]

According to the Sheffield prospectus for 1857, and in line with other British art schools, life drawing classes were for male students only. The Figure Room contained plaster casts of celebrated statues, copying which was a chief pillar of the art training Siddal had hitherto missed; so it's intriguing to think she may now have studied antique sculpture.

Much later photographs show scenes typical of art training for many decades. It also includes still-life assemblies from which students could work over weeks. There is no obvious drawing of Siddal's own invention that one can identify as being undertaken at this moment, unless it were the undated ink composition of the Macbeths. This portrays a contorted pose, as Lady Macbeth takes a dagger from her husband, who turns in a conflicted

E. E. Siddal, The Macbeths, 1858-60?

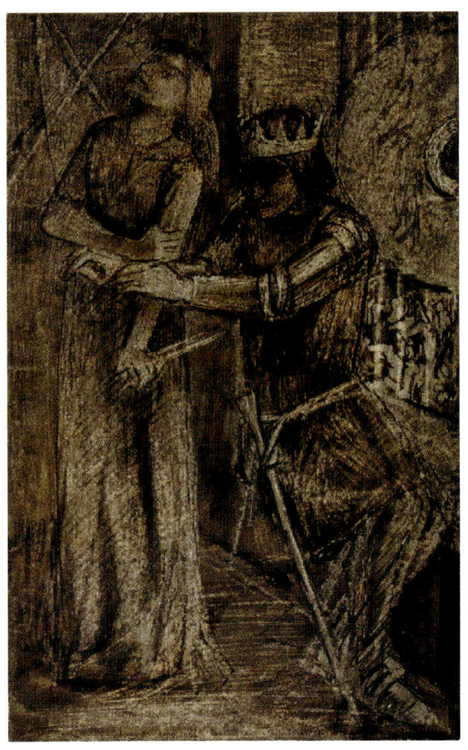

gesture of resistance and surrender. He has just killed King Duncan; she has now to finish the task to 'smear the sleepy grooms with blood'. It is a signally violent act in a violent drama, by a transgressive female character. But this may have come much later, when Siddal is known to be reading Shakespeare.

As well as her knowledge of contemporary artists, A. S. was struck by Siddal's distinctive dress style, which was so 'uncommon' that the other female students regarded it as 'unbecoming and absurd' and made jokes and caricatures about it. Again, it's hard to guess exactly how this was judged: Siddal was generally at the forefront of fashion. Flounced crinolines worn with wide pagoda sleeves may have seemed excessive to some. One of the satiric drawings fell into Mitchell's hands, 'and well do I remember how his black eyes glared round the class and the sarcastic words he threw at us'. Or perhaps Lizzie wore a hoopless, corsetless smock in what was later called a Pre-Raphaelite style, which would have been equally comical to her classmates. Soon after, on the special excursion train to Manchester, she wore a beautiful silk dress in the height of prevailing fashion.

The day trip—just over 30 miles by rail—probably took place in September. Tickets to the 'Art Treasures' cost one shilling and 16,000 works were on view. Millais, Hunt and Brown were all represented in the contemporary section, so Siddal was well placed to share with her companions personal knowledge of their work. Evidently Young Mitchell was pleased to have such a well-connected student among his flock.

D. G. Rossetti, Study for Sir Lancelot in the Queen's Chamber, 1857. This is Rossetti's first drawing of Jane Burden, posing in Oxford as Queen Guinevere

Eccleshall Road, where Siddal lodged, runs south-west towards Hathersage and the Peak District. According to Ibbitt, she visited Endcliffe woods, Wharncliffe crags and other nearby sites. In November, she moved to Matlock, a spa town beyond Chatsworth, a northern equivalent of Bath, suited to invalids. She wrote to tell Rossetti, having apparently heard from Emma Brown that he lingered in Oxford, drawing a newly discovered model who was posing as Queen Guinevere. Rossetti, still enjoying the flattery of his new followers but also exposed to the critical scrutiny of the university now the academic term had begun, promptly went north to join Siddal. He left Jane Burden in the care of William Morris.

7. MATLOCK

IF THE WEEKS in Sheffield are under-researched and ill-chronicled in Siddal biographies, the months at Matlock are virtually blank, even though she spent almost the whole time in the company of Rossetti, whose life has been thoroughly tracked. He later wrote of 'a solitary stay in the country of some length', as if he had been alone. On another occasion he wrote that 'both Lizzie and I lodged at Matlock Bank, for nearly a year'.[1] The lodgings were taken for nine or ten months, and Siddal must have stayed there throughout, from November 1857 to early September 1858. Their rooms were at Lime Tree View, a boarding house offering private apartments and family accommodation. According to its advertisements, it occupied a sheltered, south-facing spot, with a 'very pure and bracing' air, excellent water and 'scenery unsurpassed in beauty by anything else in Derbyshire'. Run by William Cartledge, it provided 'all the privacy and comfort of home upon the most reasonable terms'—a third of the rates of an hotel—and was suitable 'for persons who may be desirous of spending the winter months in an atmosphere more than ordinarily healthful'. A pony carriage was available, at 1*s* 6*d* per hour.

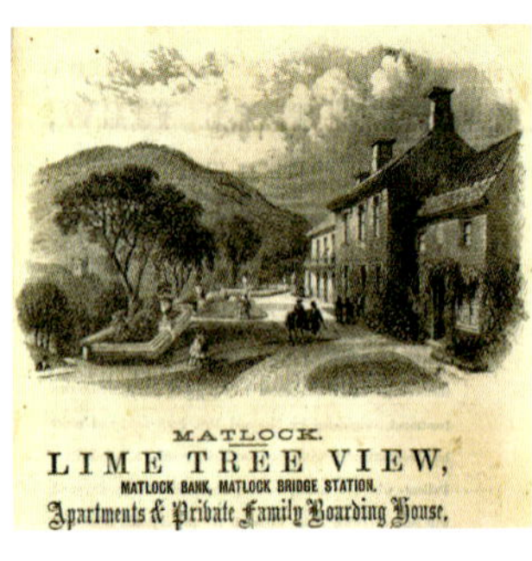

Mr. Cartledge's Lime Tree View, Matlock, seen in an advertisement of 1863. Years later, in Manchester, Cartledge fell on hard times and applied to Rossetti for assistance

And how did they spend their time in this healthful location? They had portable art materials, for sketching and colouring, and Christmas was approaching; one wonders if Siddal was prompted to return to her Nativity stable scene, which I suggested may have been conceived at Menton with the other images of the Virgin. Wrapped in blue, Mary sits by a manger holding her newborn child within her cloak. A green-clad angel stands by, fingering a musical instrument. In the preliminary sketch, the view from the thatched stable window contains three wintry trees; in the watercolour it looks more like Derbyshire, with a valley, steep hillside, animals grazing and a distant upland horizon.

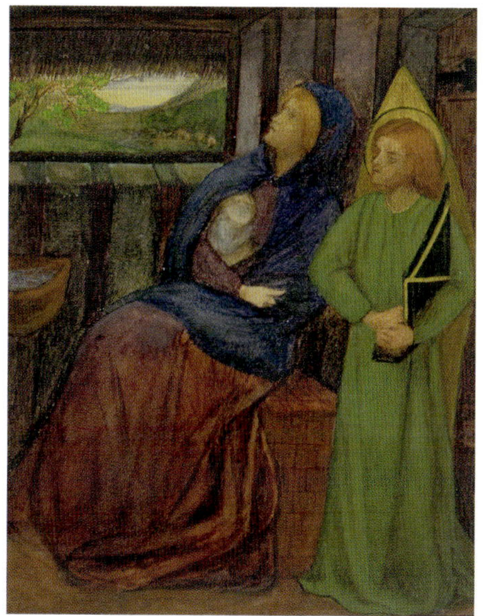

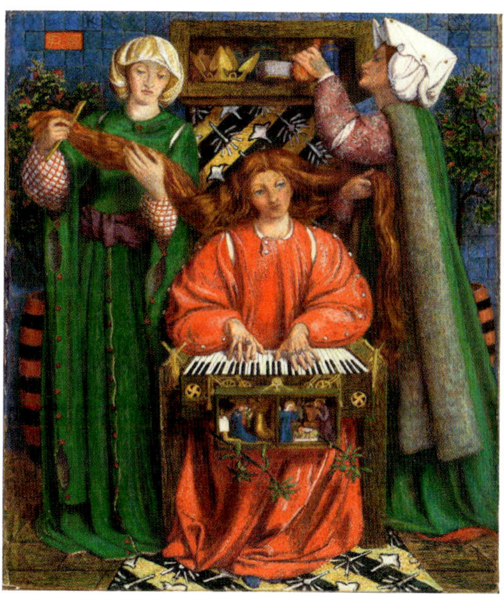

Left: E. E. Siddal, Nativity Scene, showing Virgin Mary and Christ Child, with an Angel, c. 1856

Right: D. G. Rossetti, A Christmas Carol, inscribed 'Xmas 1857–8'

This watercolour was never finished, the baby remaining in a sketchy state. But its Nativity scene was joined by Gabriel's first composition in Matlock, a topical Christmas Carol, which is inscribed 'Xmas 1857-8'. Essentially a secular image inspired by late medieval songs rather than the Gospel story, it is roughly twelve inches square, done in opaque, vivid colours reminiscent of illuminations. An auburn-haired woman is seated centre, on an archaic chair comparable to those Morris had made for the rooms at Red Lion Square. She plays a laptop keyboard whose front is decorated with small scenes of the Annunciation and Nativity, and wears a loose scarlet gown. To either side green-clad ladies comb out heavy swags of her hair. This motif, with long tresses held out sideways, is also in Siddal's designs for *La Belle Dame sans Merci*, with a knight in place of the attendant women. The central figure has Siddal's features and no doubt her slender outspread fingers, but the likeness is generic and subordinated to the highly patterned, glowing scene. It could have been a Christmas gift, but they both accepted that artworks were made for sale, so unsurprisingly it was sent for exhibition nine months later, and sold to a patron.

Rossetti also had quite another project, to complete his translations of early Italian verse that had long languished in abeyance, and which he asked Ruskin to subsidise. As well as sonnets and canzoniere by Cavalcanti and Cino da Pistoia, the project included Dante's *Vita Nuova*, which relates his adoration of Beatrice, interspersed with sonnets. These were now polished and prepared for publication. He was also reading—presumably aloud during wet days and winter evenings—from the medieval romances and histories that Morris championed: more from the *Morte Darthur*, the chansons de geste and Froissart's *Chronicles* of the Hundred Years' War, with battles and massacres and chivalric deeds.

They went on some excursions, north past Darley Dale to late medieval Haddon Hall, with its stone courtyards, great hall, panelled walls and minstrel gallery. It prompted a pair of pictures, imagining knights and ladies there. Siddal depicts a chivalric-domestic scene: a kneeling knight carefully hammers in nails to attach his lady's favour to a lance. She has one arm round his shoulders, and with the other she holds the lance steady in an image of close concentration on the task in hand. The red banner hangs between her blue skirt and his black garments and chainmail. Through a high window a moorland skyline is visible, while through a lower doorway a squire holds the horse on which the knight will ride out—to a Malorian tournament.

Just as Rossetti's Christmas image was a companion to Siddal's *Nativity*, his *Before the Battle* is a version of her Lady and Knight. Both works depict a medieval lady tying her pennon to

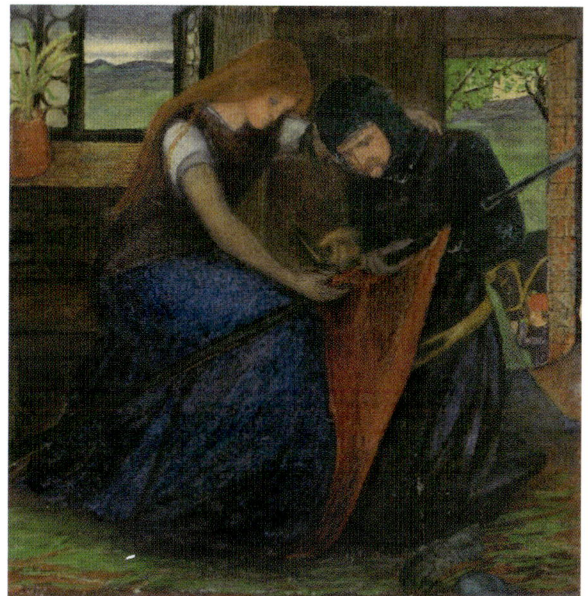

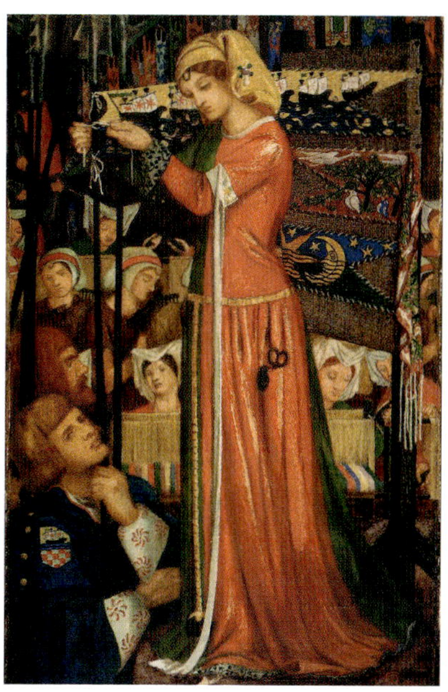

Left: E. E. Siddal, Lady & Knight preparing for a tournament, c. 1858

Right: D. G. Rossetti, Before the Battle, 1858

a long lance. Both use primary colours of vermilion and ultramarine. Siddal's is more conventionally staged, where Rossetti's adopts a radical perspective, as if the viewer stands in a high gallery alongside the woman, looking down into a hall filled with women carding and weaving banners. The main woman wears a red gown with green cloak, and ties an embroidered pennon to a vertical lance. In the background small armoured figures cluster beneath many decorated banners, in a densely packed and patterned composition, that contrasts with Siddal's airy castle interior. Both seem inspired by Haddon Hall. When later Rossetti offered his work to Norton, he outlined its subject, explaining that '[it] represents a castle full of ladies who have been embroidering banners which are now being fastened to the spears by the Lady of the castle. There are a good many figures & half figures large & small in it; and I hope that in colour it is one of the best things I have done.' Recognising that this was very different from the Dantean scene that Norton expected, he added 'These chivalric Froissartian themes are quite a passion of mine, but whether of yours also I do not know.'[2] The price was 50 guineas.

No dates can be attached to Siddal's poems, which exist only in draft form. Her reading of Tennyson, Border ballads, Scott's novels, the Brownings' poems and other contemporary fiction and verse was strong on Victorian medievalism, and her own efforts reflect this. The taste may have been encouraged by ancient buildings in Yorkshire and Derbyshire, with the implicit invitation to ignore the industrial present in favour of imagined scenes and characters from 'olden times'. Evoking actual ballads in metre and content, Siddal's dramatised 'O mother open the window wide' echoes Lord Randal, while the comparably archaic 'Earl Richard' is set beside a tomb effigy, where the speaker tells her dead lover she is about to marry:

Farewell, Earl Richard,
Tender and brave;
Kneeling I kiss
The dust from your grave.

Pray for me, Richard,
Lying alone
With hands pleading earnestly
All in white stone.

Soon I must leave thee
This sweet summer tide;
That other is waiting
To claim his pale bride.

Soon I'll return to thee
Hopeful and brave
When the dead leaves
Blow over thy grave.

Then shall they find me
Close at thy head
Watching or waking,
Sleeping or dead.

Another rehearses the familiar lament about reunion in heaven:

Ruthless hands have torn her
From one that loved her well;
Angels have upborn her,
Christ her grief to tell.

She shall stand to listen
She shall stand and sing,
Till three winged angels
Her lover's soul shall bring.

He and she and the angels three
Before God's face shall stand;
There they shall pray among themselves
And sing at His right hand.

The faint echoes of Rossetti's verses in 'The Blessed Damozel' (originally published in 1850) and 'Bridechamber Talk' (worked on around this time) are less obvious than the fact that grief and consolation are the standard motifs in Victorian verse, and that Siddal's ballad mode, with occasionally irregular metrics but a sustained tone, is the most popular in English literature. One can't prove that Siddal's fragmentary stanzas were composed in 1858, but a season of writing and sketching could have

And I have heard the night-wind cry
And deemed its speech mine own.

A little while a little love
The scattering autumn hoards for us
Whose bower is not yet ruinous
Nor quite unleaved our songless grove.

Only across the shaken boughs
We hear the flood-tides seek the sea,
And deep in both our hearts they rouse
One wail for thee and me.

A little while a little love
May yet be ours who have not said
The word it makes our eyes afraid
To know that each is thinking of.

Not yet the end: be our lips dumb
In smiles a little season yet:
I'll tell thee, when the end is come,
How we may best forget.

'Not yet the end.' But seemingly it was. Very unusually, when they were first published in 1870, these verses were explicitly dated 1859.

At unknown dates, Siddal composed her own poems on the subject, which can be considered her responses to the experience, if not to Gabriel's lines, which she may not have read. That later titled 'Dead Love' is angrily reproachful:

Oh never weep for love that is dead
Since love is seldom true
But changes his fashion from blue to red,
From brightest red to blue,

And love was born to an early death
And is so seldom true.

Then harbour no smile on your bonny face
To win the deepest sigh.
The fairest words on truest lips
Pass on and surely die,
And you will stand alone my dear,
When wintry winds draw nigh.

Sweet, never weep for what cannot be,
For this God has not given.
If the merest dream of love were true
Then, sweet, we should be in Heaven,
And this is only earth my dear,
Where true love is not given.

Gabriel's sister was impressed by the 'cool, bitter sarcasm' here. 'Love and Hate' is even more bitter, reading like a curse:

Ope not thy lips, thou foolish one,
Nor turn to me thy face;
The blasts of heaven shall strike thee down
Ere I will give thee grace.

Take thou thy shadow from my path,
Nor turn to me and pray;
The wild wild winds thy dirge may sing
Ere I will bid thee stay.

Lift thy false brow from the dust
Nor wild thine hands entwine
Among the golden summer leaves
To mock this gay sunshine.

And turn away thy false dark eyes,
Nor gaze upon my face;
Great love I bore thee now great hate
Sits grimly in its place.

All changes pass me like a dream,
I neither sing nor pray;
And thou art like the poisonous tree
That stole my life away.

Thirdly, in 'The Passing of Love' the poet laments the change from joy to anguish:

O God, forgive me that I ranged
My life into a dream of love!
Will tears of anguish never wash
The passion from my blood?

Love kept my heart in a song of joy,
My pulses quivered to the tune;
The coldest blasts of winter blew
Upon me like sweet airs in June.

Love floated on the mists of morn
And rested on the sunset's rays;
He calmed the thunder of the storm
And lighted all my ways.

Love held me joyful through the day
And dreaming ever through the night;
No evil thing could come to me,
My spirit was so light.

O Heaven help my foolish heart
Which heeded not the passing time

That dragged my idol from its place
And shattered all its shrine.

It's hard not to read these pieces as personal. But poetry is also fiction, words chosen to evoke events or emotions, dramatisations not direct transcripts of feeling. When he read them for the first time some decades later, Swinburne remarked on the 'note of originality in discipleship which distinguishes her work in art', adding that 'Gabriel's influence and example is not more perceptible than her own independence and freshness of inspiration.'[6]

Should we assume Siddal returned to her family home in Southwark after leaving Matlock in late summer 1858? William Rossetti later alluded to Lizzie's separation from Gabriel from autumn 1858 and 'the whole of 1859'.[7] James Siddall stated that 'during the later [18]50s I saw much of my sister',[8] which suggests she went home.

The fact that no friends recall seeing her suggests that the relationship with Rossetti was over. The break may have been dramatised in a verse fragment[9] found among Gabriel's discarded manuscripts:

But before going out, she took her stand
At the wide door, and struck him with her hate
Full on the cheek; and the scorn did not bate

Nor the strength failed an instant. With one hand
She heaped her fallen tresses in their band
And with the other, turning, closed the gate.

This could chime with Siddal's own lines 'Great love I bore thee: now great hate Sits grimly in its place.' If they are personally expressive, did a major disagreement lead to parting? His translations completed, Gabriel had been bored 'in these solitudes' at Matlock. At 30, he was haunted by the Italian proverb warning that 'chi a trenta non fa, mai non farà' ('what you don't do by thirty, you never will do'). He needed to return to the art world. Did he tell Lizzie so, with no mention of marriage? What of their partnership? Lizzie would reach the same age in a few months, when custom prescribed a spinster's mobcap; in a vivid novella Christina Rossetti described an unmarried woman anxiously scanning her hair on her 30th birthday for immediate signs of ageing.

They had had angry rows and arguments before. Did something made this one worse? From a later event comes a possible hint. In the mid-1860s the Rossetti brothers held a number of spiritualist 'séances'. Various friends and hired mediums took part and during two sessions, in February 1866 and August 1868, the summoned 'spirit' identified itself as Elizabeth Rossetti. William kept a careful record of the sessions, in the mode of a civil service minute-taker. On the second occasion, William, Gabriel, the studio assistant Harry Dunn, and Fanny Cornforth were present. William asked the spirit if she knew them all; yes, all except Dunn was the reply. Gabriel asked the standard questions: was she happy? Yes. Happier than on earth? Yes. After some more in this vein, he asked if she now liked Fanny? Yes. But some while ago you used not to like her? No. Did you pull her hair on a particular occasion?

Here William inserted a note of his own, confirming that this had happened: 'I was present at it.' The spirit replied Yes. To which Gabriel responded, Will you pull her hair now? Yes. Disappointingly, William also recorded that 'no such thing was actually done'. And then Fanny took her hands from the table and the tilting manifestations stopped.

Earlier, the spirit named Elizabeth had claimed not to have known Fanny personally. It is clear that Rossetti did not

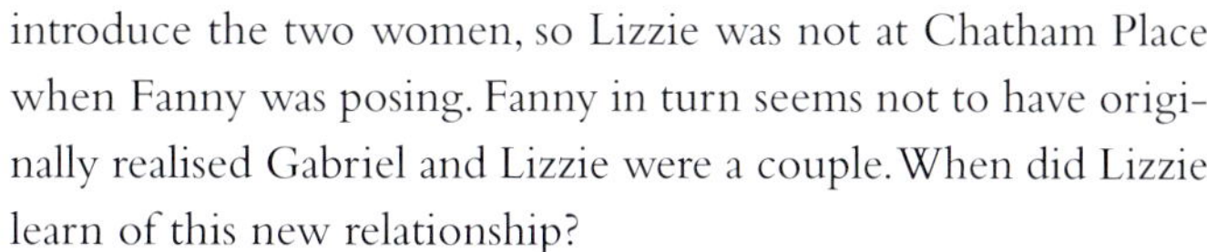

introduce the two women, so Lizzie was not at Chatham Place when Fanny was posing. Fanny in turn seems not to have originally realised Gabriel and Lizzie were a couple. When did Lizzie learn of this new relationship?

If she returned to London, she presumably went home during the winter and spring of 1859. Little is known of the Siddall family circumstances at this time. Sister Lydia was engaged to Joseph Wheeler. Their father was ailing; Lizzie and Lydia would be needed by their mother, until and after Charles Siddall's death in July. The cutlery business was inherited by their brother James, who now had to support his disabled brother Harry as well as mother and sisters.

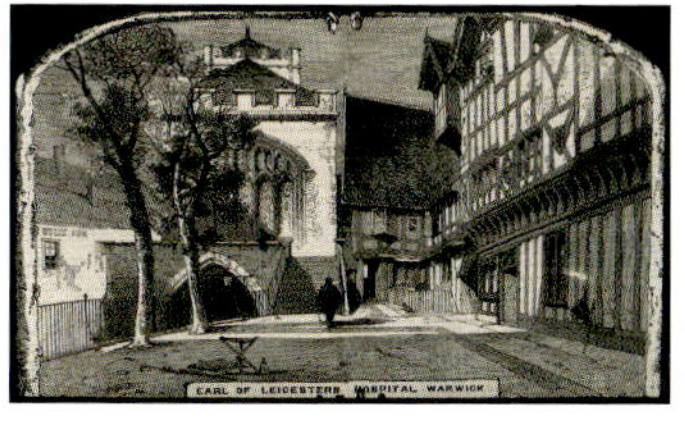

Lord Leycester Hospital, Warwick (1450), in the late 19th century

Rossetti made no mention of this in any extant correspondence. Were they still engaged? Until recently a long estrangement and Lizzie's worsening health has been supposed. Now, however, new evidence has emerged from old sources, revealing that over Christmas and New Year 1859–60, Gabriel and Lizzie were together in Warwickshire. On 23 December they visited the medieval chapel and Elizabethan buildings of the Lord Leycester Hospital in Warwick. Rossetti then returned to London—he was there on 28 December—before travelling back to Warwickshire. There they both checked into the Bath Hotel in Leamington Spa, identifying themselves as 'Mr and Miss Rossetti'. On 9 January they went to Shakespeare's Birthplace in Stratford-upon-Avon. In both Warwick and Stratford they signed the visitors' books with their usual names.[10]

So it seems that any estrangement was over. In November Rossetti had received the first payment for his triptych at Llandaff Cathedral, providing ready cash. Possibly this—and the loss of financial support from the Siddall shop—prompted renewed promises of marriage. But no date was set. Another few months passed.

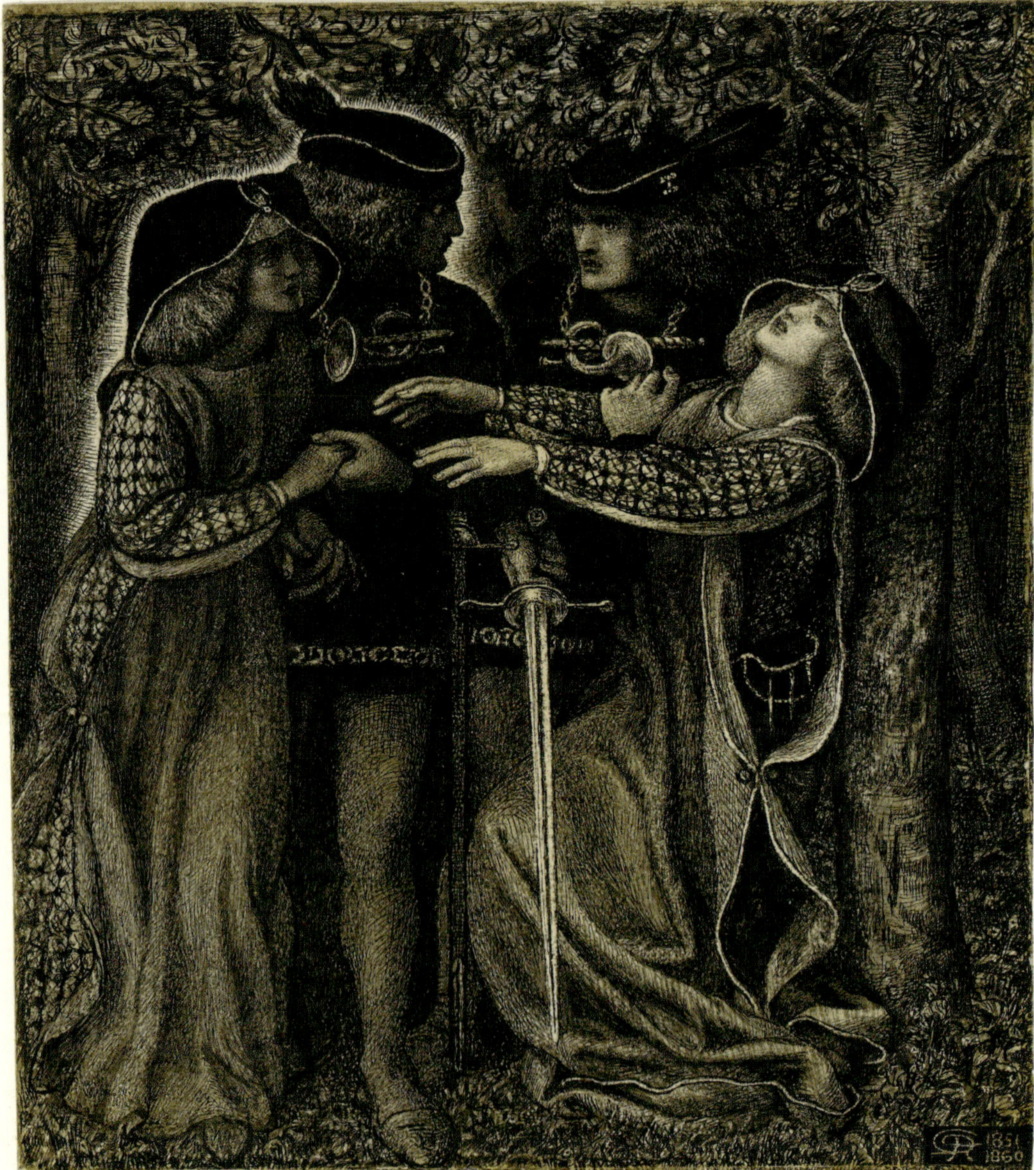
1851
1860

8. MARRIAGE

SIDDAL'S NEXT DOCUMENTED appearance was unexpected. 'Lizzy and I are going to be married at last, in as few days as possible,' Rossetti told his family on 13 April 1860. 'I have hardly deserved that Lizzy should still consent to it, but she has done so, and I trust I may still have time to prove my thankfulness to her.'[1] He wrote from Hastings, where a couple of days later he obtained a licence for the wedding to take place without waiting the normal month. This was needed because she was seriously ill, 'ready to die daily and more than once a day'. Madox Brown hastened to Hastings, with Emma's offer to help, but Lizzie wanted only Gabriel. The main symptoms were weakness, weight loss, sweating fever and continual vomiting.

Without offering a diagnosis, these symptoms are typically associated with opiate addiction, or more accurately with withdrawal from opium in its forms as laudanum and heroin. Rossetti dropped everything to look after her. A comparable situation is described in a poem to which he now returned:

> Long sat she silent; and then raised
> Her head, with such a gasp
> As while she summoned breath to speak
> Fanned high that furnace in the cheek
> But sucked the heart-pulse cold and weak.

On 21 April, a slight improvement made Gabriel feel as if he had been 'dug out of a vault, so many times lately has it seemed to me that she could never lift her head again'.[2]

One must speculate as to a sequence of events. Had there been an overdose scare? Did Lizzie or Clara send a message to Gabriel, directly or via Brown or Ruskin? Did Rossetti then escort her to Hastings, fearing she would die? If she did, he told William, 'I should have so much to grieve for, and what is worse, so much to reproach myself with.'

Opposite: D. G. Rossetti, How They Met Themselves, 1860

'We were a little taken by surprise,' William confessed. 'She is a beautiful creature, with fine powers and sweet character: if only her health should become firmer after marriage, I think it will be a happy match. At all events, I am very glad that Gabriel is settled upon it.'[3] Fanny Cornforth was not glad; when Boyce called a little while later, she was in bed, 'in a very nervous, critical state'.[4]

Much later, Lizzie's niece—Lydia's Siddal's daughter—observed that, having been in the world of artists so long, 'one could hardly imagine that she would have married some perhaps ordinary workingman'.[5] Which may point to Siddal's predicament when the relationship foundered—if it had. Now it resumed, with remorse on Gabriel's part. 'Like all the important things I ever meant to do—to fulfil duty or secure happiness—this one has been deferred almost beyond possibility,' he told his mother, without revealing whether marriage was a matter of duty or happiness.[6]

After a couple of false starts, Lizzie recovered enough for them to marry in Hastings on 23 May, the only guests being two local residents as witnesses. In Victorian times, weddings were often modest affairs, without celebrations or special clothes. Joanna Boyce married Henry Wells in this practical manner in Rome at the end of 1857. More surprisingly, given her poor health, the new Mrs Rossetti proceeded with her husband to Boulogne and then Paris, to enjoy a conventional-seeming honeymoon. Gabriel was not idle, drawing a portrait of his father's old comrade Giuseppe Maenza, with whose family he had lodged as a teenager, and composing a dense, mysterious image of themselves meeting their doubles in a dark wood. It is inscribed '1851–1860', which records the years of their meeting and marriage. Although in this sense a celebration, it is also ominous, for in folklore, to meet one's doppelgänger presages death.

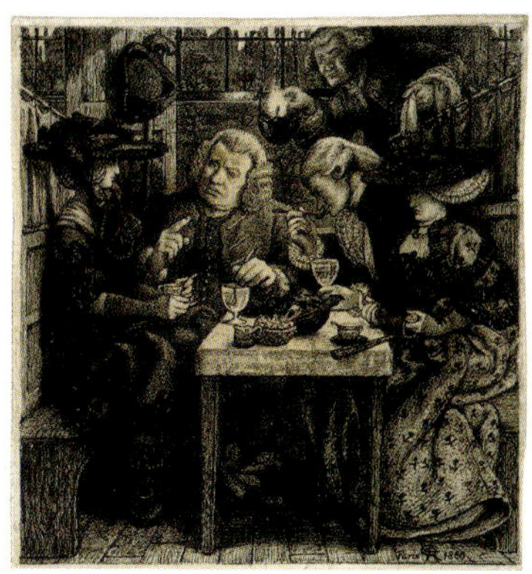

D. G. Rossetti, Dr Johnson at the Mitre, 1860

Perhaps it was defiant, Lizzie having in Gabriel's eyes just cheated death. In Paris they planned to meet the newly married Ned and Georgie Jones, who failed to arrive after Ned fell ill. Gabriel visited the exhibitions and the Louvre. Together they laughed over extracts from Pepys' Diary and Boswell's *Johnson* and Gabriel designed a comic scene of Dr Johnson flirting with two women at the Mitre. They laughed over menu mistranslations, and acquired two lap-dogs, which must be seen as a gesture of hope in the future.

What may Siddal have been drawing? A number of compositional sketches lack secure dates, including several figure studies illustrating 'La Belle Dame sans Merci' by Keats, but none with an obvious or implied link to this period. I will assume that Siddal was in a convalescent state, recovering from the near-fatal condition that had prompted the wedding. While it is very unwise to regard poems as confessional, just possibly these draft verses express her feelings, of release from near-fatal distress:

Many a mile over land and sea
Unsummoned my love returned to me;
I remember not the words he said
But only the trees moaning overhead.

[...]

How sounded my words so still and slow
To the great strong heart that loved me so,
Who came to save me from pain and wrong
And comfort me with a love so strong.

Some poetic drafts are signed 'E.E.R', which indicates composition or revision after May 1862, and thus renewed artistic energy. Quite soon she was at work on her illustration for Gabriel's long, medievalish poem 'The Bride's Chamber', structured as a ballad dialogue between sisters Aloyse and Amelotte.

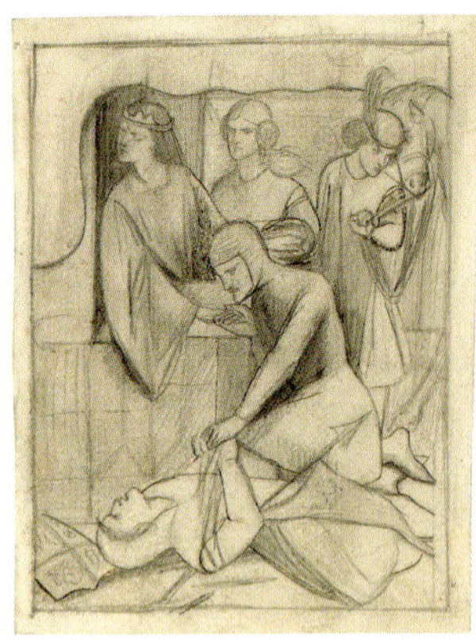

E. E. Siddal, Study for The Woeful Victory, c.1860. In a tournament, the kneeling knight has just killed his rival and claims the hand of the Lady, who hates him

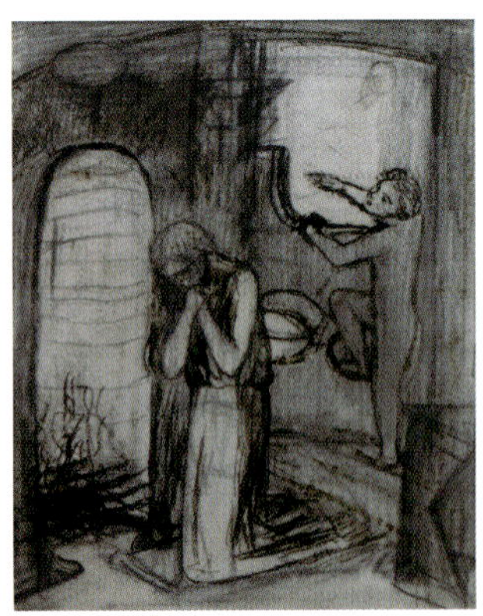

E. E. Siddal, Study for Sister Helen, unknown date. Illustrating Rossetti's ballad poem in which Helen avenges her betrayal by means of sorcery

The drawing entitled *The Woeful Victory* depicts a version of his planned plot-line involving a tragic tournament. Later, the poem was further complicated; at this date the storyline focussed on the heroine's dismay when her beloved knight is killed by his dark rival, whom she must now marry.

Possibly, too, she returned to another illustration, to Rossetti's poem 'Sister Helen', for which a number of compositional ideas survive. The text, which Gabriel was revising for publication, presents a ballad in which Helen casts a spell that kills her faithless lover, as witnessed by her brother—a Gothick tale in keeping with the spooky stories that so enchanted the whole circle.

Returning to London, after what one friend called Gabriel's 'matrimonial escapade',[7] they took lodgings in Hampstead, not far from Keats' house. It was customary for new married couples to pay calls and send out cards, but with their bohemian ways Lizzie and Gabriel deemed this 'all too much trouble, you know'.[8] Moreover, when in August they were invited to the Rossetti home for the evening, together with Ned and Georgie and Mrs Bell Scott, Lizzie was too ill to attend and therefore again failed to meet her in-laws, who as well as sisters Maria and Christina included Gabriel's aunts Margaret and Eliza and probably his cousin Henrietta. As Letitia Scott reported, 'Mrs Gabriel Rossetti has not yet been seen in his mother's house, and has been invisible to everybody.'[9] This was distinctly disrespectful, and clear proof of the lack of welcome Lizzie received from the Rossetti women. With thinly veiled disapproval, Christina wrote that Gabriel's marriage 'would be more of a satisfaction to us if we had seen his bride; but owing I dare say in great measure to the very delicate state of her health, we have not yet met.' She meant in their new formal relationship, adding frostily: 'some years ago I knew her slightly: she was then extremely admired for beauty and talent' but ending more warmly with 'I hope we shall be good friends some day.'[10]

From her use of 'I dare say', it is evident that Christina was unaware that Siddal was not necessarily 'ill' but pregnant, with a baby that must have been conceived in July. The subject was virtually taboo in conversation and correspondence, either from delicacy or fear of misfortune, so friends and family were often left in ignorance. Then, by the time it was unignorable, social life was more or less suspended for a pregnant woman.

Although she did not pay a courtesy call on his family, Lizzie met her husband's new friends, when the Joneses were invited with the Browns to join a visit to the Zoo in Regent's Park—'place of meeting The Wombat's Lair'—and to dine at Spring Cottage, their Hampstead lodgings. This was an event for Georgie, who was in awe of Lizzie's reputation, both for talent and elegance. She recalled how tall and slim Lizzie was, dressed in a smart jacket over her crinoline—Georgie being very small and soberly clad. At Spring Cottage,

> I see her in the little upstairs bedroom with its lattice window, to which she carried me when we arrived, and the mass of her beautiful deep-red hair as she took off her bonnet: she wore her hair very loosely fastened up, so it fell in soft, heavy wings [...] Whilst we were in her room she shewed [*sic*] me a design she had just made, called 'The Woeful Victory'.[11]

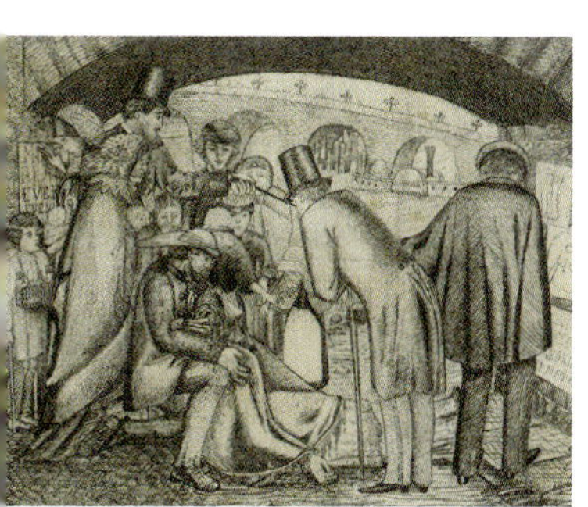

G. [Burne-] Jones, The Bridge of Sighs, 1860. Illustrating Thomas Hood's poem on a destitute woman's suicide.

When they next met, Georgie could have shared her own image, of a drowned woman retrieved from the Thames, illustrating 'The Bridge of Sighs' poem.

One day the young couples went to Hampton Court and lost themselves in the maze. They also met up with William and Jane Morris, who had just moved in to their newly built home,

Bexley in Kent. Jane was as tall and slender as Lizzie, dark-haired and very shy. Eleven years younger and a stableman's daughter from Oxford, she was no doubt also awed by Lizzie's sophistication. The Morrises were expecting their first child in January. Hoping they would all socialise as married couples, Rossetti wanted also to introduce the Wellses, who now had two infants and lived in Kensington.

During the day, Gabriel travelled in to Blackfriars, to carry on painting at Chatham Place. He took responsibilities seriously, even as far as to seek portrait commissions, which were the bedrock of professional practice.

Lizzie's pregnancy stammered; two medical men were summoned. When the alarm subsided, she went to Brighton with Lydia. From here she wrote to reassure Gabriel, in one of her few letters to survive in full. 'My dear Gug,' it began,

> I am most sorry to have worried you about coming back when you have so many things to upset you. I shall therefore say no more about it. I seem to have gained flesh within in the last ten days, and also seem much better in some respects, although I am in constant pain and cannot sleep at nights for fear of another illness like the last. But do not feel anxious about it, as I would not fail to let you know about it, and perhaps after all I am better here with Lyddy than quite alone at Hampstead. I really do not know what to advise about the little house in the lane. If you were to take it, you might retain your rooms at Chatham Place, which I think would be the best thing to do until better times. However I do not see how the £30 are to be paid just at this time, so I suppose that will settle the matter. I am glad you have written to Marshall, but fear there is no chance of his being in town at this time of year.

I should like to have my watercolours sent down if possible, as I am quite destitute of all means of keeping myself alive. I have kept myself alive hitherto by going out to sea in the smallest boat I can find. What do you say to my not being sick in the very roughest weather? I should like to see your picture when finished, but I suppose it will go away somewhere this week. Let me know its fate as soon as it is sealed and pray do not worry yourself about it as there is no real cause for doing so. I can do without money till next Thursday, after which time £3 a week will be quite enough for our wants, including rent of course.

Your affectionate Lizzie.[12]

Reading this, one is struck by the similarity of tone and content in the letters between Joanna and Henry Wells this season, when Henry was professionally away painting commissioned portraits. Both are conjugal exchanges rather than love letters. They read as affectionate and practical, giving posterity no clue as to any estrangement. Nor do they illuminate the nature of 'another illness like the last'. Was this the threatened miscarriage, or the earlier near-fatal collapse? It was sufficiently diminished for Lizzie to travel, enjoy a boat trip and resume drawing—all despite constant pain and insomnia. A second surviving letter from this time is in the same style, with quotidian details that cannot be elucidated, nor need to be.

My dear Gabriel, I am most sorry to think of your picture going at that low price but of course there was nothing else to be done. I wish you would put aside or send on to me the money for those knives, as I do not wish those people to think I am unable to pay for them. The price of the knives is two shillings each.

your affectionate Lizzie.

(As a cutler's daughter, Siddal would know about knives. One would like to know who 'those people' were from whom she had ordered them. And how many? dining, carving or painting knives?—at two shillings apiece they must have been well-tooled and sharpened.)

It is unclear which of Rossetti's pictures had been sold; his newest customer was Thomas Plint, an enthusiastic stockbroker who had commissioned Brown's *Work*. Most likely the picture was the fanciful *Wedding of St George and Princess Sabra*, which imagines the martial saint marrying the princess he rescued from the dragon. In a confined picture space the couple embrace, as Sabra snips a lock of her black hair to tie onto George's helmet. They sit in two basket-weave chairs, with the dragon's body lying supine. It was described as:

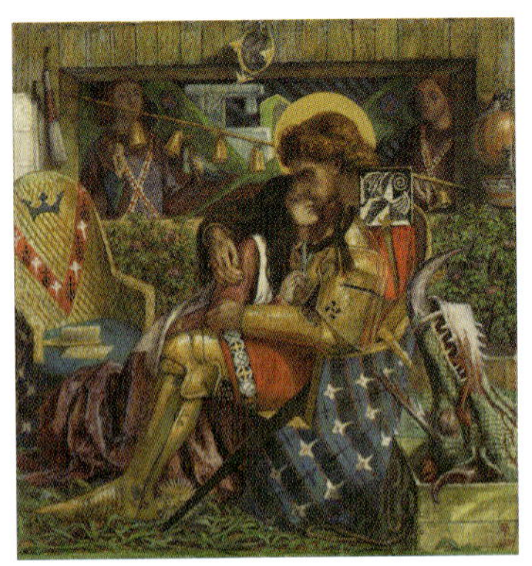

D. G. Rossetti, The Wedding of St George and Princess Sabra, 1857–60. One of several designs featuring the legend of St George

> one of the grandest things, like a golden dim dream … a sense of secret enclosure in 'palace chambers far apart' but quaint chambers in quaint palaces where angels creep in through sliding doors, and stand behind rows of flowers, drumming on golden bells, with wings crimson and green. There was also a queer remnant of a dragon's head which he had brought up in a box (for supper possibly) with its long, red, arrowy tongue lolling out so comically, and the glazed eye which somehow seemed to wink at the spectator, as much as to say 'Do you believe in St George and the dragon? If you do, I don't, but do you think we mean nothing, the man in gold and I?'[13]

Rossetti earned 55 guineas for this, which could have paid for dozens of knives, and many weeks' rent in Brighton.

The Woeful Victory, Siddal's own image this season, was more conventionally medieval. A more complex group than any she had hitherto produced, set within a perspectively compressed

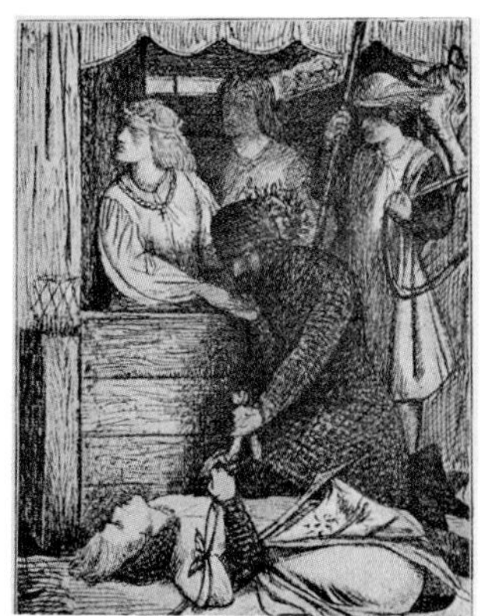

E. E. Siddal, The Woeful Victory, 1860

picture space, the five figures are all of similar size despite standing in different planes. In the foreground lies a recumbent knight in chainmail whose shield has tumbled by his head and whose slender spear is attached to a pennon with a coronet device. Behind this a kneeling knight in chainmail bends over the fallen one, whose joined hands he clasps in his left hand while his right touches that of a lady behind a low masonry wall, while somehow in the same plane far right are the hoof and head of a horse held by a squire wearing a feathered cap. To the left we see the lady wearing a coronet and a gown with wide sleeves; she turns away from the kneeling knight who holds her right hand while her left hand reaches back and across to that of an attendant female turned left, with a dove on her shoulder. Lady and attendant occupy a sort of high-backed settle with a wavy top-rail, which also pictorially contains the squire and horse.

Drafts of this crowded composition reveal the work in progress. A study in pencil with the figures in outline is now in the Cecil Higgins Museum Bedford (p. 114). Another, now unlocated, version shows the knights and ladies grouped to the right and slightly receding, with a horse's head, neck and two awkward front legs on the left edge. Then (and this is the order in which Rossetti placed them when making a posthumous album of photos of all Siddal's sketches) a third ink image returns to the first composition, with the slain knight in front, helmet off and fair hair outspread, hands tied by a rope held by the kneeling knight, behind whom stands the squire, holding a lance and the reins of the horse, on the far right. The ladies are now within a timber pavilion hung with curtains and their attendant in deep shadow. The whole has much detail and textural patterning, while the figures, so tightly bunched, are more 'correctly' rendered with perspective and shading.

In the romance-poem 'Bridechamber Talk' that Rossetti

began for *The Germ* in 1849 and developed in 1858-60 as 'The Bride's Prelude', the tale unfolds as a dialogue between sisters Aloyse and Amelotte, in which Aloyse relates her unhappy history with the knight Urscelyn and the birth and apparent death of the resulting baby. Annotated 'Part One', the Prelude ends in a plague year, as Aloyse ends her confession:

> And often in that year
> Of plague and want, when side by side
> We've knelt to pray with them that died
> My prayer was 'Show her what I hide!'

The proposed sequel in which Urscelyn reappears and determines to marry Aloyse, was only schemed out in prose, with variant details, as for example

> Amelotte wd draw attention to the passing of the time. Aloyse then says—There is much now you remember—how we heard that Urscelyn had become a soldier of fortune and how he returned here. You must also remember with the death of that young knight at the tourney. Amelotte should then describe the event & say how well she remembers Urscelyn's bitter grief at the mischance. Aloyse wd then tell her how she herself was betrothed herself to the young knight & how Urscelyn slew him intentionally. As the bridal procession appears, perhaps it might become apparent that the brothers meant to kill Urscelyn when he has married her.[14]

This draft continuation, transcribed a decade later, fits the Woeful Victory scene, and thus raises the question as to whether it was adopted in response to Siddal's design, or at her suggestion, in another instance of artistic collaboration? Which takes us back to the days at Matlock, when both were working on

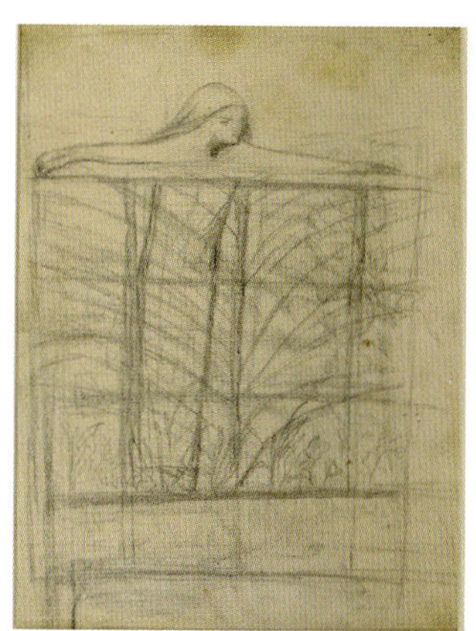

E. E. Siddal, Study for The Blessed Damozel, 1855. The Damsel leans from the bar of Heaven to watch her beloved on Earth

'chivalric' compositions. Encouraged by completing his Italian translations, and by the reprinting of his 'The Blessed Damozel' in *The Oxford & Cambridge Magazine*, Rossetti also revived his ambition to publish a volume of original verse. It has always been assumed that Siddal's sketches illustrating his early poems—'The Blessed Damozel' and 'Sister Helen'—were composed in the early years of their relationship. Certainly a design for 'Sister Helen' dates from 1854, but did she return to this and the Damozel when Gabriel returned to his texts? If so, they may have been intended as illustrations to the projected original volume, alongside 'The Bride's Prelude'.

If so, again, this may relate to Siddal's activity during the 'lost' months of 1859. An alternative narrative from the end of the time at Lime Tree View could see Siddal living independently, as she had done in Menton and Sheffield, while Rossetti resumed his familiar life at Blackfriars. Perhaps she had plans to rejoin him in spring 1859, only to find that his life and art had moved on, under what one may term a 'Venetian' influence, and that companionate marriage was no longer high on the agenda, at least not until the Warwickshire interlude.

James Siddall later told William Rossetti that 'it was well-known in the family that my sister was given to fits of melancholy'. Such 'fits' sound like depressive episodes, which must date from this period, as in the mid-1850s she had scarcely lived at the Siddall home. While insisting that he was aware of nothing beyond 'the common misunderstandings' between couples, James added that, during these occurrences, 'there would be nothing extraordinary in a man like Rossetti—the poet and painter—withdrawing himself for the moment'.[15] This implies there was a rupture. Or was this James's response to a question from William?

Unwise as it is to read poems as 'love personals', the

temptation is strong when so few autobiographical items exist. Siddal's draft verses include two lyrics of lost love and implicit suicidal longing. One begins:

It is not now a longing year
That parts us, not a day
Yet the green leaves touch me on the cheek
Dear Christ this month of May
Yet who can take their first dear love
And kiss him the old way?

Variant stanzas exist in manuscript, one copied out by Gabriel, presumably from a lost draft, which invokes feverish or psychotic hallucinations:

Dim phantoms of an unknown ill
Float through my tired brain;
The unformed visions of my life
Pass by in ghostly train
Some pause to touch me on the cheek
Some scatter tears like rain
A silence falls upon my heart
And hushes all its pain.
I stretch my hands in the long grass
And fall to sleep again,
There to lie empty of all love
Like beaten corn of grain.

Another deploys the Tennysonian tropes of mourning, together with religious imagery of reunion in a fractured, unpunctuated sequence:

Life and night are falling
from me, Death and are

opening on me,
wherever my footsteps
come and go life is a
stony way of woe
Lord, have I long to go?

Hollow hearts are ever
near me, soulless eyes have
ceased to cheer me
Lord may I come to thee?

Life and youth and summer
weather to my heart no joy
can gather
Lord, lift me from life's stony way.

Loved eyes long closed in death
watch for me holy death is
waiting for me
Lord, may I come to-day

My outward life feels sad
and still like lilies in
a frozen rill
I am gazing upwards to the
sun, Lord, Lord, remembering
my lost one
Oh Lord, remember me

How is it in the unknown
land do the dead wander
hand in hand
give me trust in thee.

Do we clasp dead hands

and quiver with an endless
joy for ever
good be unto thee
[...]
Do tall white angels
gaze and wend along
the banks where lilies
bend

Lord, we know not how
this may be good Lord
we put our faith in thee
Oh God, remember me.

Although unstructured, these verses seem too thoughtful for a writer in the debilitated condition that Siddal's state in spring 1860 indicates. One may conjecture however, that the deteriorating relationship with Rossetti in 1859, allied to her father's death, which removed a basic pillar of support, together with pain-numbing opiate use, may have led to the physical collapse that by the following Easter occasioned the long-delayed marriage. All speculation, of course, but how easily can one account for the swiftness of their wedding and the smoothness with which they settled into married life, almost as if there had been no rift?

Much later Georgie pondered the issue. 'The question of her long years of ill-health has often puzzled me,' she wrote; 'how was it possible for her to suffer so much without developing a specific disease?'[16]

But now things seem to go well, as the letters from Brighton suggest. When she returned to London, they looked for another house; failing to secure an eligible one in Hampstead's Church Row, they decided instead to rent the adjacent apartment at 13 Chatham Place, thus allowing the existing studio at No. 14 to continue in use. 'We now have a suite of 6 rooms,' Gabriel announced, 'including a spare bedroom for a friend.'[17] True to their bohemian credentials, they preferred serviced lodgings to the responsibilities of a household with servants to supervise. At Chatham Place Mrs Birrell, the housekeeper, managed domestic services like hot water, coal fires, cleaning and probably laundry, while meals were brought in or eaten out. Mrs Birrell's niece Ellen Macintyre was employed as maidservant, sleeping in the original apartment while the new couple set up home as it were next door, with Siddal's watercolours in gilt mounts hung round the 'drawing room', where guests were entertained. The Parisian dogs seem to have soon been given away, but Lizzie acquired a songbird.

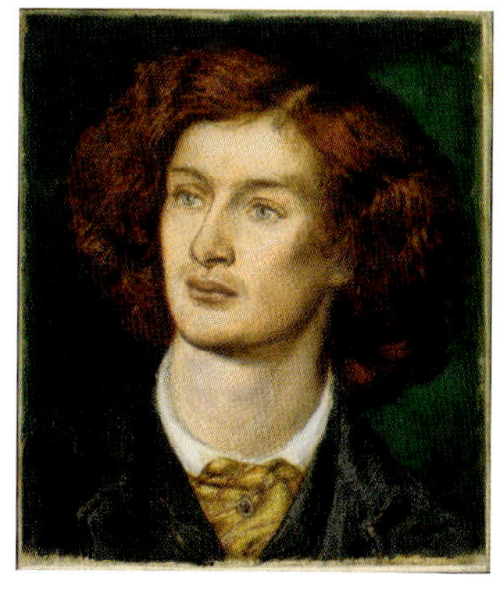

D. G. Rossetti, Algernon Swinburne, 1861

On return from his summer travels Ruskin called with congratulations. Anna Mary Howitt introduced her husband Alaric Watts, Henry Wells brought Joanna, Jane and William Morris were invited to stay over after an evening visit from their home in Kent. Siddal met other friends of Gabriel, including Algernon Swinburne, who would later become her champion and with whom the young couples went to see *The Colleen Bawn*, the theatrical hit of the season by Dion Boucicault, with its melodramatic plot and spectacular stage effects. It ran for 350 performances. Georgie recalled the programme seller's dismay at two red-heads in the same row, the hair colour being superstitiously regarded as unlucky.

Few biographers have wondered whether the coppery colour of Siddal's hair influenced her self-esteem. 'Carrot top', 'Ginger nut', 'freckleface' were the kind of casual insults common on the streets when she was a child (bonnets and shawls hid adult women's hair in public), which could have fostered a degree of defiance, reflected in her abrasive, chaffy manner.

9. DEATH

'INDEED AND OF COURSE my wife does draw still,' Rossetti assured Norton on 29 November 1860.

> Her last designs would, I am sure, surprise and delight you, and I hope she is going to do better than ever now. I feel surer every time she works that she has real genius—none of your make-believe—in conception and colour; and, if she can only add a little more of the precision in carrying-out which it so much needs health and strength to attain, she will, I am sure, paint such pictures as no woman has painted yet.

But, he added with greater caution, 'it is no use hoping for too much'.[1]

Referring to 'designs' in plural implies that *The Woeful Victory* was not the only new work. This could relate to the plan for Lizzie and Georgie to write and illustrate a book of uncanny tales, modelled on those by the Brothers Grimm (which the Burne-Joneses joked were 'truly grim'). Georgie sketched out some ideas, including one in which instead of her own likeness the heroine sees Death in a mirror, but no textual drafts by Lizzie have survived. Georgie told Ruskin of her ambition to create woodblock versions of Ned's drawings, which he regarded as a commendable wifely project, and which echoed Lizzie's illustrations to Gabriel's poems. 'Sister Helen' would have been an appropriately macabre tale.

They went to the Morrises' Red House at Christmastime, where the whole group of friends was drafted in to decorate walls and ceilings. In the large drawing room Ned began murals illustrating the medieval romance of Sir Degravaunt, which concludes with the wedding feast for Degravaunt and the Lady Melidor, whose images he based on Morris and Jane. In a bedroom Gabriel, Brown and Siddal undertook a figure frieze depicting biblical characters that feature in Voragine's *Golden Legend*, a medieval favourite for Morris.

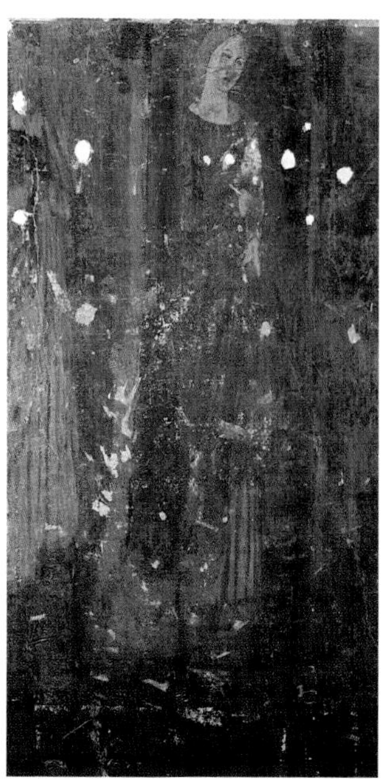

E. E. Siddal, Rachel, 1860. Damaged remains of mural depicting figures from the Book of Genesis, at William Morris's Red House

The Red House mural, painted so as to resemble a wall-hanging or tapestry, contained tall figures of Adam and Eve by Rossetti and Noah by Brown, together with Rachel and Jacob. Siddal is thought to have painted Rachel and perhaps Jacob too, with his iconographic ladder. The decoration, painted on to new plaster, never very robust, then damaged and for decades hidden from view, is now almost wholly decayed, making authorship conjectural. The depiction appears stiff and inept, but was in fact relatively sophisticated, devised to mimic the folds of a tapestry curtain, so sections of the figures are unseen. The large scale, too, was a departure from Siddal's usual miniature images. Her endeavour was in good company, if one recalls the comparable fate of the murals in the Oxford Union by Rossetti, Burne-Jones, Morris and the rest. At Red House Jane and other female members of the group stitched large needlework panels based on Chaucer's *Legend of Good Women*. Despite her dressmaking experience, embroidery was never recorded as one of Siddal's skills.

All Victorian women, however, had their 'work' and its equipment of pins, needles, thread, scissors and thimble, in a needlework bag or box or basket, on hand for darning, mending, sewing on buttons and stitching garments. Making clothes and covers for babies and infants occupied much maternal time, even after the arrival of the first sewing machines in 1860. Georgie was the grateful recipient of one, as a wedding present from G. F. Watts, but recalled how at Red House she and Janey spent their mornings mending and making by hand.

The whole group were also full of high spirits, playing games and making jokes. In emulation of Edward Lear's *Book of Nonsense* came the group's passion for limericks, usually invoking the most unlikely notions as well as the most awkward names. Ned Jones was rhymed with 'edged-uns', meaning sharp tools. Demure Georgie was said to 'indulge each night in an orgy'. She recorded how Gabriel began one limerick with the lines: 'There is a poor creature named Lizzie, Whose aspect is meagre and frizzy,' only for Lizzie to trump it with her own, using as rhyme-word the colloquial term for sixpence:

> There is a poor creature named Lizzie
> Whose pictures are dear at a tizzy;
> And of this great proof
> Is that all stand aloof.
> From paying that sum unto Lizzie.

(a pound was a 'quid', a shilling a 'bob' and a half-shilling or six-pence a 'tizzy').

Jane's daughter, always known as Jenny, was born at Red House in January, with Emma Brown in support. The friends gathered again for her baptism on 21 February 1861, followed by a convivial meal on trestle tables in the wide entrance hall. Georgie recalled that she and Rossetti drank only water, she owing to her Methodist background, he because unlike most of the fellows, he never drank alcohol or smoked tobacco.

Though her presence is not recorded, it is likely that Siddal was there too, and had been to stay previously, for a fragment of a letter survives. 'If you can come down here on Saturday evening, I shall be very glad indeed,' she wrote. 'I want you to do something to the figure I have been trying to paint on the wall, but I fear it must all come out, for I am too blind and sick to see what I am about.'

At Blackfriars, they also had decorative plans, inspired by Red House. Delft tiles with their naïve blue designs were set round the fireplace, complementing antique blue-and-white willow pattern porcelain, the latest enthusiasm. 'Our drawing room is a beauty,' Gabriel told Allingham; 'we shall have it newly papered from a design of mine which I have an opportunity of getting made by a paper manufacturer somewhat as below.' A rough ink sketch of spindly trees followed:

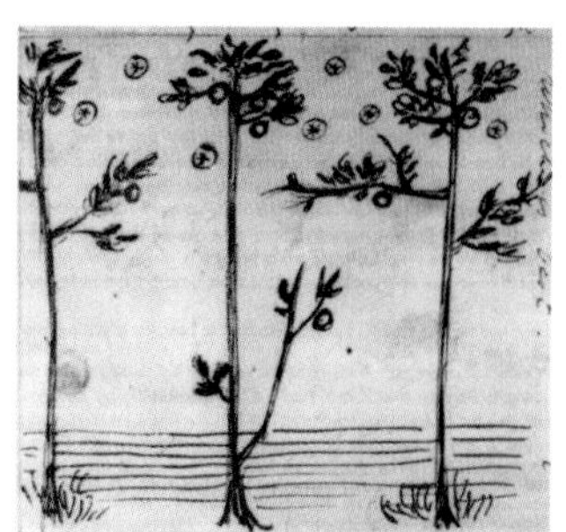

D. G. Rossetti, Sketch of projected wallpaper design, 1860, for the apartment at Chatham Place. 'Rather sombre, but rich'

> I shall have it printed on common brown packing paper and on blue grocer's paper, to try which is best [...] The trees are to stand the whole height of the room, so that the effect will be slighter and quieter than in the sketch where the tops look too large. Of course they will be wholly conventional. The stems & fruit will be Venetian Red — the leaves black. The fruit however will have a line of yellow to indicate roundness & to distinguish it from the stem. The lines of the ground black. And the stars yellow with a white ring round them. The red & black will be made of the same key as the brown or the blue ground so that the effect of the whole will be rather sombre but I think rich also. When we get the paper up we shall have the doors & wainscotting painted summer house green.[2]

The design partly echoes the *Golden Legend* mural, where stylised trees separate each figure. Though never executed, the wallpaper plan arose from another scheme, a decorating business inspired by the Red House interiors. Chiefly executed by Morris with his characteristic dispatch, this was conceived in January 1861 and established by April. Constituted as Morris, Marshall, Faulkner & Co., it was 'an association of architects and painters, who have set up a shop in Red Lion Square, in the same manner as the Italian painters, such as Giotto, did in the Middle Ages'.[3] In modern terms, it was a design partnership, offering goods and services to ecclesiastical and domestic customers. Rossetti was a partner, along with Brown, Jones and the architect Philip Webb; as professionals rather than tradesmen, these four withheld their names from the firm's business title, but undertook most of the commissions, designing stained glass windows, mural patterns, tiles, furniture, wallpaper, table glass and church embroidery, work being and allocated at weekly meetings. As well as producing two major window sequences for the tales of *Tristram and Iseult* and *St George and the Dragon*, Rossetti was especially active in promoting the business. He was also active on his own account, with several small pictures to accompany work on the Llandaff triptych and the resumed canvas of *Found*, for which Fanny Cornforth had posed during the hiatus in the relationship with Lizzie. In March, he returned to teaching an evening class at the Working Men's College, conveniently also in Red Lion Square, just over a mile north of Blackfriars. In addition, he was busy with literary projects. Christina was enlisted to copy out the manuscript of the Early Italian translations, which then received final revisions and introduction before being set in type, together with an attractive illustration of an embracing Renaissance couple and a projected author's portrait. This was ready for publication in May, albeit without illustrations. More or less at the same time came a collection of original verses, for a volume to be titled *Dante at Verona and Other Poems*. These were copied into a soft leather-bound red-edged notebook, together with the latest version of the 'Bride's Prelude', and circulated to Allingham and Ruskin for comments. They included the three pieces that Siddal had begun to illustrate.

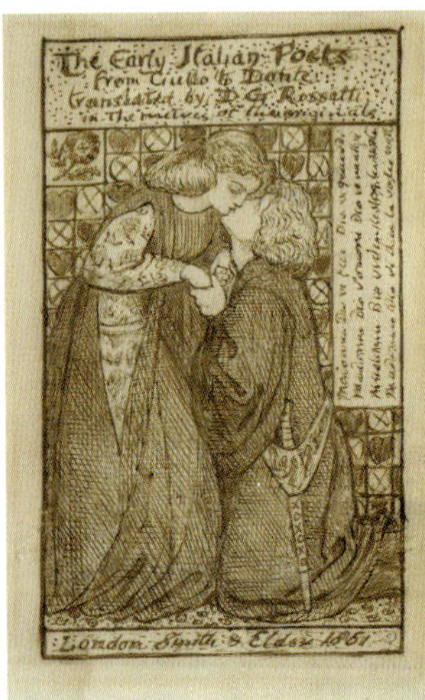

D. G. Rossetti, title-page design for his translations of Italian poems, issued in 1861 without the design. Algernon Swinburne posed for the kneeling figure

Additionally, this year Gabriel made efforts to get Christina's poems into print, urging them on Ruskin and publisher Alexander Macmillan. 'Really, they must come out somehow', he told his sister.[4] One evening early in February, at Blackfriars ,he read some of her work with his own to some literary friends. Christina then forwarded manuscript copies to the publisher Alex Macmillan, with Gabriel's promise to illustrate 'Goblin

Market'. A little while later, Rossetti met Alexander Gilchrist, whose biography of William Blake he eagerly assisted, having many years previously acquired one of Blake's notebooks. All this activity signified a new determination to further his professional career, as artist, author, designer, husband and prospective father. It must also have meant that Siddal was often on her own at Chatham Place, stitching baby clothes, preparing a cradle, resting. Perhaps because of their marital harmony she was not regarded as needing special care. There are hints of creative activity, including the two poems initialled 'E E R'. She also began to decorate a Gothic-style wooden box, which can be associated with the launch of the Firm.

Now at Kelmscott Manor, this is known as Jane Morris's jewel casket. Jane's daughter May, who as a child enjoyed handling both box and contents, recorded that its decorative panels with scenes of medieval ladies and lords were painted by Rossetti and Siddal—information that evidently came from her parents. Owing to this history, it was assumed that the casket was a gift to Jane, as a present on her wedding in 1859. But Liz-

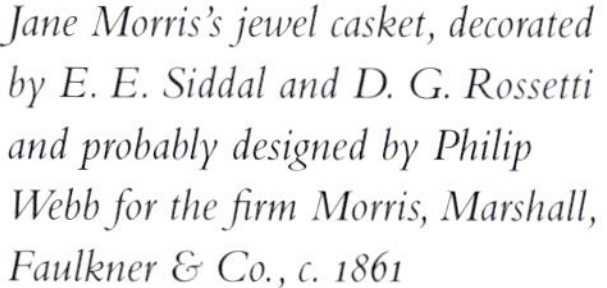

Jane Morris's jewel casket, decorated by E. E. Siddal and D. G. Rossetti and probably designed by Philip Webb for the firm Morris, Marshall, Faulkner & Co., c. 1861

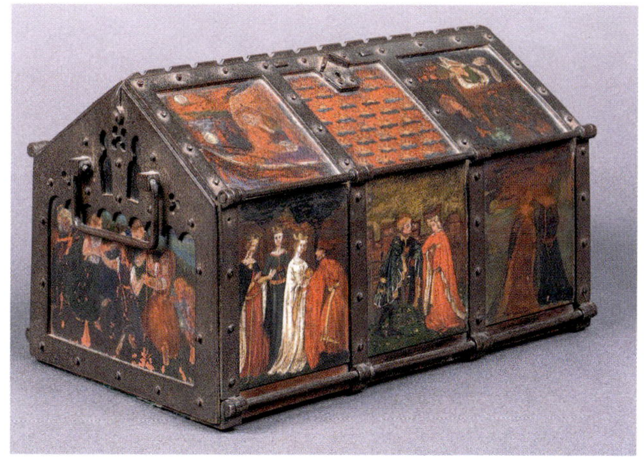

zie met Jane 16 months later; the casket was probably made in 1861; and the decoration is unfinished. It is unlikely to have been a wedding gift. Moreover, the design of the box, modelled on medieval reliquaries, with gabled ends and a hinged lid, is now ascribed to Philip Webb, who was the Firm's principal designer of furniture, an attribution that makes sense. Painted cabinets were among the Firm's earliest products, shown at the 1862 exhibition. It is plausible, therefore, to see the box as a possible prototype, decorated in the same medievalising mode as the St George cabinet and panelled Gothic chest designed by Webb and to propose that the casket dates from the same moment, and was Siddal's decorative project.

For in its origins, the Firm was a collective endeavour. Embroideries were stitched by Georgie, Jane and Elizabeth Burden, Jane's sister; tiles were painted by Kate and Lucy Faulkner, sisters of the Firm's accountant. The jewellery casket has 14 small panels, of which seven are painted, mainly with courtly scenes derived from medieval illuminations, notably a manuscript version of Christine de Pisan's *Cite des Dames*, known as the *Book of the Queen* in the British Library collection. Siddal and Rossetti knew and used these sources and at least one of the jewel box images is copied from a depiction of the Choice of Paris there. Others, particularly three of the more sketchily painted panels link pictorially to Siddal's drawings and draft—figures in a skiff with a full moon, a medieval blessed damozel gazing down on her love, and two women in a landscape setting. These are very clearly unfinished.

Sometimes the friends gathered at Blackfriars. One of Siddal's few surviving letters was kept by Georgie, whom she addressed as 'my dear little Georgie', on account of her small stature:

> I hope you intend coming over with Ned tomorrow evening like a sweetmeat—it seems so long since I saw you, dear. Janey will be here. I hope to meet you
>
> With a willow pattern dish full of love to you and Ned
>
> Lizzie.[5]

As was customary for those with the means, a maternity nurse was engaged, to care for mother and baby during the first month. But, fatefully, she was not required. In April, the child stopped moving. Two medical men were consulted. 'We can but wait and trust for a happy termination,' Gabriel told friends. But the symptoms indicate that placental abruption, as it is now termed, had taken place, causing death in the womb, followed in a few weeks by a stillbirth—in this case a daughter. 'Lizzie has just been delivered of a dead child,' Gabriel sadly reported on 2 May.[6] The only consolation was that her own life was not in jeopardy.

Childbirth in the Victorian era was notoriously dangerous, especially due to obstetric infection or puerperal fever. The causes of placental abruption are still unknown, although today fœtal monitoring and swift intervention by a cæserean can save the child's life. Protracted sorrow frequently follows a stillbirth.

Both parents were afflicted. Gabriel would mark the anniversary 'dies atra'—black or fateful day—and used the imagery of stillbirth in later poems. The hour 'which might have been yet might not be' features in 'Stillborn Love', while 'Death-in-Love' describes a feather being held 'to lips that stirred it not [...] Behold, there is no breath'. When he suffered a paranoid breakdown, he imagined their daughter's ghost whimpering in the next room. Lizzie too was immediately desolated. When Georgie and Ned called, she was rocking the empty cradle and put her fingers to her lips: 'Hush, you'll waken her.' But she wanted Georgie to have the baby's 'small wardrobe' of clothes. Please 'Don't let her, please,' Gabriel wrote, 'it looks such a bad omen for us.'[7] The maternity nurse stayed on for her month. Swinburne called regularly. Lizzie was unable to go to the 'great Pre-Raphaelite crush' as Mary Howitt described an evening hosted by Mrs Seddon on 13 June, attended by 'Joneses, Morrises, Browns', Holman Hunt and his sister, George Boyce, Henry Wells and a dozen more.[8] 'Their pictures covered the walls and their sketchbooks the tables,' Howitt told her daughter. 'The uncrinolined women, with their wild hair, which was very beautiful, their picturesque dresses and rich colouring, looked like figures out of the Pre-Raphaelite pictures.' Rossetti lent a folio of sketches, so Siddal's image was present even if she was not. He hoped to take her to the Royal Academy show, although Joanna Wells' enchanting picture of nursemaid and baby playing 'Peep-bo!' would surely have been distressing—as was the news in July of Joanna's own death from fever following the birth of her third child. 'All people who are at all happy or useful seem to be taken away,' Lizzie wrote to Gabriel, adding that Joanna's death would be 'a fearful blow' to Henry Wells, 'for she must have been the head of the firm and most useful to him.'[9] This acute comment reveals how for some couples marriage was seen as an artistic as well as domestic partnership, and that Lizzie correctly assessed Joanna Wells' leading role.

The letter also suggests she seemed to be recovering, although not sufficiently to be left alone, for she wrote while staying with the Browns. Here, their daughters recalled her sitting motionless, staring into space. She left abruptly, upsetting Rossetti with her unexpected return. The sources don't say so, but grief and agitation were no doubt quelled with laudanum. Georgie recalled that she was restless whenever Gabriel was out of the room, seeming only to calm down when with him. Later, he would say she could not have lived without laudanum.

Georgie's son Philip was born on 1 October. Some while later, Lizzie and Janey called at the same time to see mother and baby in their apartment opposite the British Museum. 'They were as unalike as possible and quite perfect as a contrast to each other,' Georgie wrote:

> Also at the time neither was under the cloud of ill-health. The difference between them maybe typified as that between sculpture and painting. Mrs Morris being the statue and Mrs Rossetti the picture. The grave nobility of colourless perfection in the one [Jane] was made human by kindness [...] while a wistfulness that often accompanied the brilliant loveliness and grace of the other [Lizzie] gave an unearthly character to her beauty'.[10]

But when the women were together, Lizzie did not chatter.

Gabriel had commissions to fulfil, and debts to pay because Thomas Plint died, his executors then demanding repayment of advances totalling 680 guineas. In November he took Lizzie to stay at Red House, while he went to paint portraits in Yorkshire. Once again, she left without warning, heading to Blackfriars. Gabriel asked his mother to take round some cash urgently. There are hints that his family were more concerned for him, caring for an invalid while having many commissions to fulfil. Published in December, his anthology *Early Italian Poets* was well received, *The Athenæum* commending the editor-translator of 'a handsome, an original and a very interesting volume'.

Using Siddal's signature motif of a small, high window, Rossetti painted her as the Princess Sabra in another image of

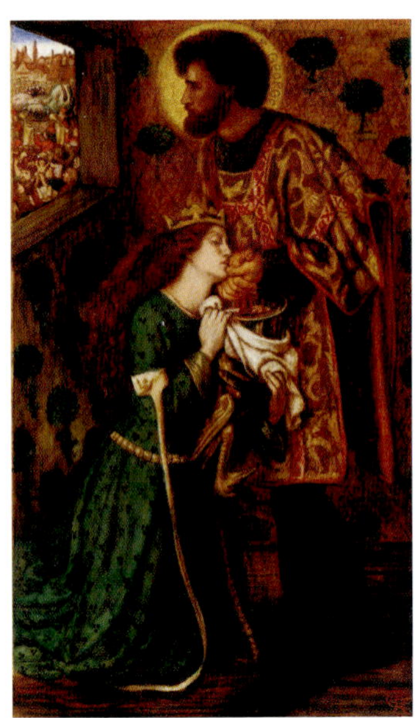

D. G. Rossetti, St George and Princess Sabra, 1862. The last picture for which Elizabeth Siddal posed, in December 1861

the St George story. Through the window a jubilant crowd fills medieval city streets, carrying the dragon's gigantic body. Inside the chamber, whose walls are covered with versions of the Red House mural patterns, St George rinses blood from his hands using his upturned helmet as a basin. Kneeling, Sabra holds helmet and towel, her lips to his hands. A commission from a friend of Ruskin, this was on the verge of completion by Christmas, having been delayed, as Rossetti explained 'by other work, and also by my wife's delicate health making it difficult for her just now to sit for me'. However, she had now done so, and the result was 'strictly one of my best drawings', price 65 guineas. A month later, Lizzie sat also for the figures of Beatrice, enrapt, and of Ophelia, distracted. The result was hardly a likeness, but a visual invocation of mental derangement. But she herself seemed better, ordering a new mantle or cloak to wear outdoors.

Meanwhile Morris and the partners at the Firm committed to displaying its work at the 'International Exhibition' which was planned for May 1862, although threatened by the sudden death of Prince Albert. 'We mean to do wonders—indeed are already making some way,' Rossetti told Norton in January. 'I wish you could see a painted cabinet, and other furniture of great beauty, which we have in hand [...] of course the plan is to effect something worth doing by co-operation, but without in the least interfering with the individual pursuits of those among us who are painters.'[11] Sadly, these hopes no longer included Siddal. If the jewel casket was intended for the Firm, it had been laid aside, half-decorated.

'I used to come and read to her sometimes,' recalled Swinburne, citing the Jacobean comedy *The Spanish Curate*, in which curate and sexton miraculously remember a supposed old friend when ducats are forthcoming. 'I can hear the music of her laughter to this day.'[12] With Gabriel they laughed too over a collection

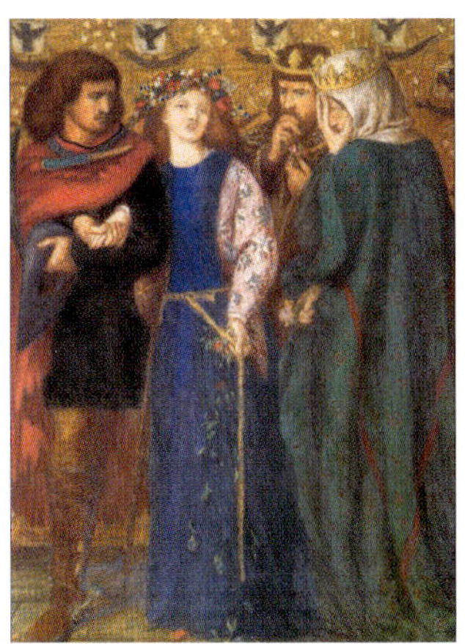

D. G. Rossetti, The First Madness of Ophelia, 1864

of traditional ballads, including the Laird o'Warristoun, in which lord and lady argue:

> He spak a word in jest;
> Her answer wasna good;
> He threw a plate at her face,
> Made it a' gush out o' blood.

and in retaliation she strangles him.

All seemed relatively stable. On 8 February, Clara called round in the evening. On Monday 10 February, about four in the afternoon, housekeeper Mrs Birrell saw Lizzie, perhaps to take up hot water or coals, later reporting that Lizzie was then 'quite cheerful'.[13] Soon after this, with Gabriel and Swinburne, Lizzie went to dine, at a restaurant in Leicester Square once home to William Hogarth and latterly a hotel favoured by Italian exiles. In the cab, Lizzie seemed sleepy, but insisted on continuing; during the meal, her mood fluctuated between 'drowsiness and flightiness'. Back at Blackfriars by 8.00 pm, she was nervous. Gabriel left her getting ready for bed, attended by Ellen Macintyre, who was there at about 8.30 when Lizzie 'seemed cheerful'. Gabriel went off to his class at the Working Men's College, returning home around 11.30, to find Lizzie unconscious, snoring loudly. Alarmed, he summoned the nearby Dr Hutchinson, who, recognising the symptoms of an overdose, prepared a stomach pump, while Gabriel sent messages to other doctors, including surgeon John Marshall, a friend of Brown's, and to the Siddal home. When Clara arrived, he set off to fetch Brown. Hutchinson stayed till 6.00 am, when he left Lizzie in Marshall's care, still utterly unresponsive.

At twenty minutes past seven in the morning, she died. 'The poor thing had been in the habit of taking laudanum for 2 or 3 years past in considerable doses, and on Monday she must have taken more than her system could bear', William reported to Fred Stephens.[14] 'I went down directly I heard it,' Georgie told her sister, 'and saw her poor body laid in the very bed where I have seen her lie and laugh in the midst of illness.'[15] A day or so later, Gabriel was seized with the conviction that Lizzie was in a death-trance and might be revived. Or perhaps that was how his grief was interpreted. Preparations were made for burial in the Rossetti plot in Highgate Cemetery where Gabriel's father had been laid, but before burial came the inquest, at the Bridewell coroner's court, on 14 February.

Called as first witness, Mrs Sarah Birrell said she had seen Lizzie asleep at about 11, and then again when summoned by Gabriel. She added:

> She used to take laudanum occasionally to produce sleep for the last twelve-months[.] I saw a phial of it was under her pillow. I knew of no hurt to her, nor don't suspect any. Her husband and herself lived very comfortable together.

Huchinson stated he had attended Lizzie's confinement the previous year:

> The child was born dead and had been dead for a fortnight before it was born. I have only seen her about once since then, that was about a month ago in the street. I was sent for on Monday night about ½ past 11. She was in a comatose state—we tried to rouse her, but without any avail. She could not swallow anything. I used the stomach pump but it had no effect. I then injected several quarts of water into the stomach and washed the stomach out. The smell of laudanum was very distinct, 100 drops is a large dose. I stayed with her till 6 in the morning [...] I believe that she died from the effects of laudanum which must have been a very large dose. The phial found in the room was about

> a 2 oz. phial. It was labelled 'Laudanum Poison'. She was in a very nervous condition when I saw her. Her husband appeared very much attached to her.

The aim of the inquest before coroner and twelve jurors was to establish circumstances and cause of death, specifically whether natural, accidental, suicidal or intentional. Hence questions about her state of mind and relationship.

'She had not spoken of wishing to die,' Gabriel stated:

> She had contemplated going out of town in a day or two and had bought a new mantle the day before. She was very nervous & had I believe a diseased heart. My impression is that she did not do it to injure herself but to quiet her nerves. She could not have lived without laudanum. She could not sleep at times nor take food.

Clara stated that on the previous Saturday, her sister had been 'in tolerably good spirits', then added:

> I was sent for and saw her about 3 on Tuesday morning. She was then alive but quite unconscious. I know of no harm to her. I don't suspect any. I heard she had taken a few drops of laudanum in brandy and water before she went to bed.

Mrs Birrell's daughter said she had previously bought a shillingsworth of laudanum for the deceased, and that the phial found was 'about half full', but she herself had not seen Lizzie take any.'I know of no hurt to her,' she concluded. 'I waited upon her and they lived very happily together.'

The verdict was that death was caused 'accidentally and casually and by misfortune'. Thus, Swinburne reported, 'the worst chance of all was escaped'. The worst being, one infers, a verdict of suicide, with its burden of blame and unconsecrated burial.

He told the inquest of dining with Lizzie and Gabriel the evening before, when he noted 'nothing particular in the deceased except that she appeared a little weaker than usual'. But he also told his mother that 'happily there was no difficulty in proving that illness had quite deranged her mind'. This is unmentioned in the coroner's report. Who, in the court, spoke of such derangement? And why invoke a 'worst case' that did not apply, unless there was a real possibility of suicide?

Some certainly thought so. John Marshall told his family that Lizzie died from 'poison she took herself. They had only been married only 2 years & she found herself superseded & took laudanum.'[16] While this is partly garbled hearsay, recounted years later, it accords with what Brown's daughter Lucy told her own daughter—that Lizzie had pinned a scribbled note to her nightgown, asking Gabriel to 'take care' of her mentally impaired brother, and that after consulting Brown, Gabriel had destroyed the note. A note, of course, would indicate suicide. Lucy also claimed to hear another friend of her parents say 'Thank God for Gabriel!' in response to the news—though this could have referred to the verdict rather than to Lizzie's death. And others besides Bell Scott must have believed that Lizzie had, in his words, 'put an end to her troubles' by overdosing. This assumption would lay a burden of guilt on Gabriel.

I don't think at this remove we can judge whether or not she intended to die, but it's worth noting that people suffering from suicidal depression may feel it is the only way to escape unbearable emotions, and thus risk the known effects of opiate overdose.

The inquest verdict cleared the way to the funeral. Few details are recorded, except that shortly before the coffin was closed, Gabriel took the red-edged notebook that contained fair copies of what had already been advertised as *Dante at Verona and*

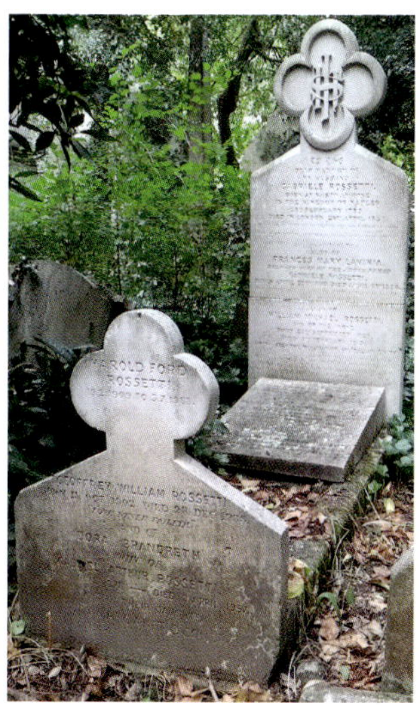

The Rossetti family grave, Highgate Cemetery

Other Poems and placed them by Lizzie's cheek, saying he had often been writing and revising the verses when he could have been attending to her. Brown protested, but William demurred, saying the gesture was honourable.

The burial took place on Monday 17 February, just a week after Lizzie's death. Gabriel seems to have been too distraught to take part; together William and Brown managed the business. At the time, it was deemed inappropriate for women to attend funerals. Gabriel could/would not return to Chatham Place; Clara and Lydia must have taken Lizzie's clothes and possessions, leaving her art-works for Gabriel to move to his new home, up river in Chelsea. Later he would vehemently reject the prospect of being buried in the same grave.

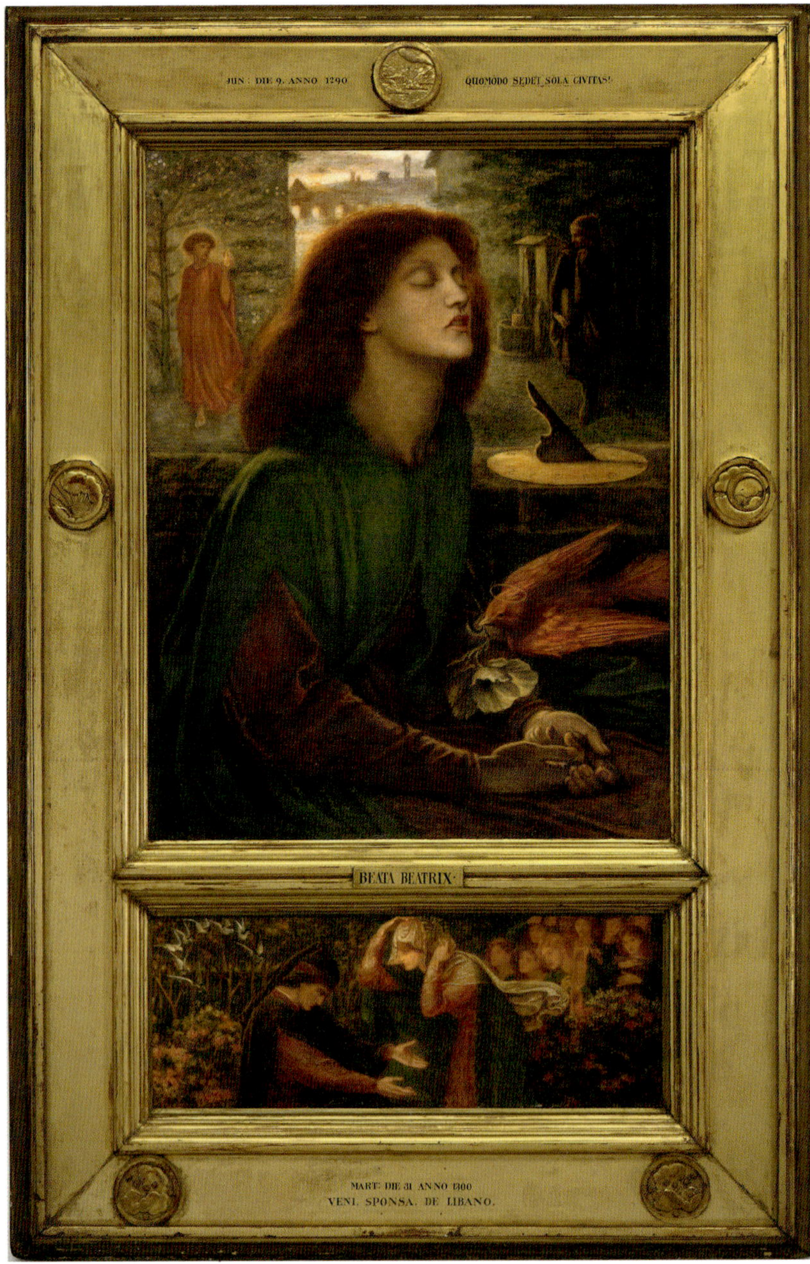
JUN : DIE 9. ANNO 1290
QUOMODO SEDET SOLA CIVITAS!
BEATA BEATRIX·
MART: DIE 31 ANNO 1300
VENI. SPONSA. DE LIBANO.

10.
EPILOGUE

THIS IS WHERE ELIZABETH SIDDAL'S life story closes, strictly speaking. Almost everything recorded in correspondence and memoirs by those who knew her has been quoted here; everything else is interpretation and imagination.

But there is a famous, myth-enhancing sequel to the burial. Six years later, when Rossetti and Janey Morris began their unwise love-affair (the subject of quite another story) he felt his eyesight failing, and returned in some panic to his poetic vocation. Prompted by the composition of odes and sonnets invoking new love, this led to a belated first volume of verse, an extension of the earlier collection in the buried notebook.

So far, so unexceptional. But some texts consigned to the coffin were unique versions—importantly the dramatic monologue 'Jenny' about a student's relationship with a prostitute that Rossetti had begun two decades earlier, and had radically re-drafted in 1858–9. Laments about the lost version led to thoughts of recovery. The notebook lay above the corpse, so could be simply retrieved if the coffin were opened. Lizzie's body would be undisturbed. It was a macabre idea, but Gabriel and Lizzie herself shared a taste for macabre tales. Moreover, as Gabriel reasoned, Lizzie had cared for poetry more than for most other things. Publication would have pleased her—perhaps would please her, if Spiritualist séances did validate messages with the dead.

D. G. Rossetti, Beata Beatrix, 1872. A memorial to Siddal, envisioned as Dante's beloved Beatrice passing from earthly life to heaven. The image was so popular with both Rossetti and his patrons that he painted three copies, adding to this version a predella depicting Beatrice and Dante meeting in Paradise

He had grieved for her. At his new house all her watercolours were mounted and framed and hung on the walls—including *Clerk Saunders,* which the Nortons had relinquished. Every drawing, study, sketch and scrap had been photographed, printed up and pasted into folio volumes, as a memorial. And for years he had worked on a memorial painting, showing Siddal as Dante's beloved Beatrice, at the moment of death and transition to heaven. And he had endeavoured to contact her through the séances, to ascertain whether she was happy in the afterlife, whatever that might be. So he had paid his widower's dues.

The truth is, he wrote:

> No one so much as herself would have approved of my doing this [...] had it been possible to her, I should have found the book on my pillow the night she was buried and could she have opened the grave no other hand would have been needed.[1]

So the project was launched, although it proved quite tricky. Exhumation was regulated, to prevent grave-robbing. Permits had to come from the grave-owner—in this case Mrs Rossetti, whom Gabriel did not wish to inform—and from the state in the form of the Home Secretary. Luckily, the latter was the Henry Bruce with whom Rossetti had negotiated the Llandaff commission, and who obligingly authorised the book's removal from the coffin, one dark evening in autumn 1869. Charles Howell, a new untrustworthy friend, took charge of logistics. The cemetery required a lawyer to ensure nothing else was taken, and a medical man supervised the drying and disinfecting of the pages. To Rossetti's dismay, 'Jenny' had large wormhole through the paper.

Digging up Lizzie's body resulted in new myth—notably that her shining red hair had continued to grow until it filled the coffin, and that like an early saint, her corpse remained undecayed. Others emerged in time, one macabre claim merging exhumation with the posthumous painting of Beatrice, to assert that Rossetti had painted his wife in death, propped up in the studio. Thus the many legends about Elizabeth Siddal were passed down to posterity.

Opposite: J. E. Millais, Study for the Head of Ophelia, 1852

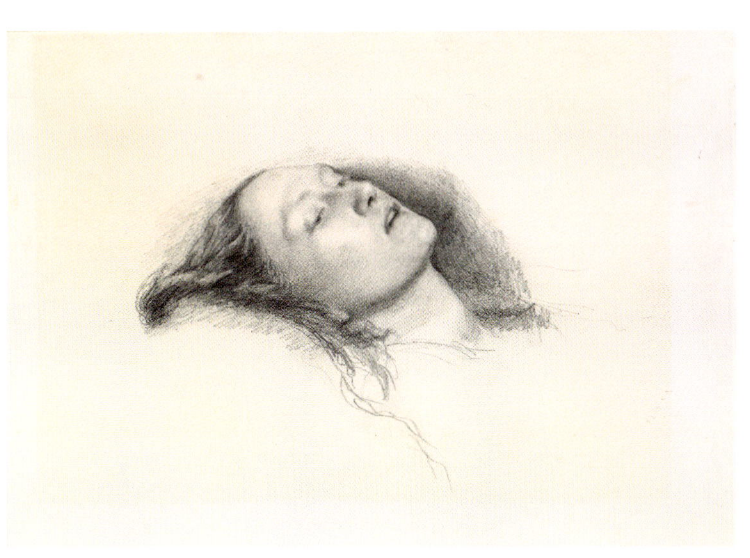

ACKNOWLEDGEMENTS

This book is dedicated with thanks and affection to David Elliott, longtime friend and publisher, responsible for issuing *The Legend of Elizabeth Siddal*, in which I first investigated the myths.

Innumerable others have since then contributed to the growing interest in Siddal's life and work, which continues. Those to whom special thanks are due in respect of this book include Rupert Maas, Alison Smith, Margaretta Frederick, Hannah Squire, Marion Edwards, Carol Jacobi, Serena Trowbridge and Alexander Fyjis-Walker, together with all those in museums and libraries who provided illustrations. Diligent efforts have been made to ascertain and contact owners and sources of unlocated illustrations. The author and publisher welcome corrections and amendments to the information given here.

As ever, heartfelt gratitude to Harry for lifetime love and support.

NOTES

PREFACE

1. Ibbitt 1862
2. WMR 1903 (2)

CHAPTER 1

1. DGR Letters 55.45
2. Arthur Hughes, quoted JGM 1899, vol. 1, 144
3. WMR 1903 (2), 273
4. Ibbitt 1862
5. *Twelfth Night* was shown at the Portland Gallery in Regent St, the *British Family* at the Royal Academy, at that date in the National Gallery building in Trafalgar Square
6. *The Times* 13 May 1851
7. See n. 4
8. See n. 4
9. Scott 1892, I, 316
10. DGR Letters, 54.55
11. WMR 1895, vol. 1, 173–4
12. WA 1907, 144
13. DGR Letters, 52.08
14. DGR 'First meeting of Dante and Beatrice'; exh. OWCS winter 52; sold to H. T. Wells
15. Knight, 1887, 71
16. J. E. Millais to W. H. Hunt 4 November 1852, quoted Holman-Hunt 1969, 92
17. WHH 1905, 1, 198–9

CHAPTER 2

1. DGR Letters 52.19
2. Boyce 2019, ii, 995
3. Howitt 1889, 340
4. Lee 1955, 216
5. Undated letter, CUL Add. MSS 7621/70, f. 307
6. Arthur Hughes, quoted JGM 1899, I, 144
7. DGR Letters 53.40
8. DGR Letters 53.48
9. Three copies of *Pippa Passes* are known: one version with an arched top signed and dated 'EES / 54', with provenance via the Rossetti family; another now at Wightwick Manor; a third possibly originating with Ruskin from the collection of John Bryson, now Ashmolean
10. DGR Letters, 54.01
11. DGR Letters, 54.29
12. Bessie Rayner Parkes to Barbara Leigh Smith, 17 April 1850, Parkes Papers 6/5, Girton College Library
13. Barbara Leigh Smith to Bessie Rayner Parkes, 1854, Troxell Collection, Princeton University Library
14. Barbara Leigh Smith to Bessie Rayner Parkes, May 1854, MSS v. 172, Girton College Library
15. DGR Letters 54.49
16. *The Athenæum*, May 1854, 278
17. Anna Mary Howitt, 'Sisters in Art', *Illustrated Exhibitor*, July 1852
18. Volumes with her name on the flyleaf are in William Morris Gallery and Fitzwilliam Museum
19. DGR Letters 54.55
20. DGR Letters 54.32

CHAPTER 3

1. DGR Letters 54.55
2. FMB Diary 6 October 1854
3. DGR Letters 55.4
4. WMR 1899, 65–6
5. Later, Fairfax Murray told William Rossetti that Charles Howell had copies of two principal pen & ink drawings by Siddal, 'viz of the "Pippa Passes" & the unknown subject with "n*ggrs" alluded to in your article' and that Howell claimed these had been made for him in DGR's studio by Dunn or Knewstub, although Howell was never to be believed (to WMR 16 Nov 1888, UBC)
6. WMR 1899, 69

7. WMR 1899, 81. EES lodged nearby, not in the Acland home
8. Atlay 1903, 228.
9. Cook and Wedderburn, 1909 vol. 36, 216
10. Cook and Wedderburn, 1909 vol. 36, 217
11. DGR Letters, 55.04
12. DGR Letters, 55.33
13. FMB Diary, 7 Aug 1855
14. FMB Diary, 6 Aug 1855
15. FMB Diary, 23 Sep 1855

CHAPTER 4

1. *The Saturday Review* 1 December 1855
2. Scott 1892, vol. II, 30
3. *Graham's Magazine*, 1855, p. 95
4. WMR 1899, 107
5. John Ruskin to Ellen Heaton, 30 December 1855
6. James Henry Bennet, *Mentone and the Riviera as a winter climate*, London 1861
7. WMR 1899, 61
8. WMR 1899, 60-62
9. William Miller, *Wintering in the Riviera, with Notes of Travel in Italy and France, and Practical Hints to Travellers*, London 1877, 207-10
10. WMR 1899, 118-121
11. Quoted Holman-Hunt 1969, 152-3
12. FMB Diary, 20 April 1856
13. FMB Diary, 14 March 1856
14. Marillier 1904, 51

CHAPTER 5

1. JGM, I, 52; FMB Diary, 17 May 1856
2. July 1856
3. WMR 1895, I, 93. WMR dated this remark to around 1857
4. Eland House, 15 Rosslyn Hill.
5. DGR Letters, 57.13
6. DGR Letters, 57.14
7. FMB Diary, 16-19 March 1857
8. Boyce 2019, I, 38
9. Boyce 2019, I, 33
10. *The Athenæum*, 11 July 1857
11. *The Saturday Review*, 4 July 1857
12. Norton 1913, I, 175
13. DGR Letters ,57.36
14. John Ruskin, *The Political Economy of Art,* lectures 10 and 13 July 1857
15. WMR 1899, 167-8
16. DGR Letters, 57.39
17. EBJ Memorials 1904, vol. I, 160

CHAPTER 6

1. Clara Siddall possibly worked at Evans mantle warehouse in Old Change Buildings
2. After EES's death it was returned by the Nortons to DGR; and inherited by WMR in 1882. In September 1884 it was purchased for £25 by Fairfax Murray, who later presented it to the Fitzwilliam Museum
3. Document by Isabella Gilchrist (1869-1947), 18 May 1928, Sheffield Local Studies Library. Gilchrist also stated that Ibbitt and Siddal were cousins. In 1803 Margaret Siddall was witness to the wedding of a William Ibbitt and widowed Ann Hodskin, who is presumed to have been sister to Margaret Siddall
4. Document by WMR 18 August 1911, Sheffield Local Studies Library
5. Document by 'A. S.', Sheffield Local Studies Library

CHAPTER 7

1. DGR Letters, 78.179
2. DGR Letters, 58.16
3. Trowbridge 2018
4. Boyce 2019, vol. II, 1022
5. Christina Rossetti to William Rossetti, 18 August 1858, *The Letters of Christina Rossetti*, ed. A. Harrison, 1997, vol. I, no. 97

6. A. C. Swinburne to WMR 4 December 1895 BL Mss Ashley 1427
7. WMR 1903 (2), 284
8. Grylls, 87, citing Helen Angeli
9. 'the cloud before the storm', Baum 1931, 62
10. G. E. Battersby 2022, citing the discoveries by Norma Hampson in the archives of Lord Leycester Hospital and Shakespeare Birthplace.

CHAPTER 8

1. DGR Letters, 60: 07
2. DGR Letters, 60: 09
3. William Rossetti to W. Bell Scott, 14 May 1860, *Selected Letters of William Michael Rossetti*, ed. R. W. Peattie, 1990, #71
4. Boyce 2019, 1040
5. Violet Hunt, notes of conversation with E. E. Higgins, transcribed 16 March 1930, Cornell University Library
6. DGR Letters 60.07
7. J. P. Seddon, quoted in *Friends of Llandaff Cathedral Annual Report*, no. 43, 13
8. DGR Letters, 60.40
9. Scott 1892, ii, 60
10. Christina Rossetti to Pauline Trevelyan, 27 August 1860, *The Letters of Christina Rossetti*, ed. A. Harrison, 1997, vol. I, no. 120
11. EBJ Memorials 1904, vol. I, 208
12. WMR 1899, 246
13. *Letters of James Smetham*, ed. S. Smetham and W. Davies, 1892, 102. Originally dated 1857, the work was designed either in Oxford or Derbyshire and was exhibited at Liverpool in autumn 1858, soon after Rossetti left Matlock. The Princess has Jane Burden's colouring
14. See MS 49323, Taylor Collection, Princeton University Library
15. Grylls 1964, 94, quoting Angeli
16. EBJ Memorials, I, 219
17. DGR Letters 61.05. This comprised the original rooms—studio, living room and bedroom, plus new drawing room, bedroom and spare room

CHAPTER 9

1. DGR Letters, 60.54
2. DGR Letters, 61.05
3. DGR Letters, 60.30
4. DGR Letters, 61.08
5. EBJ Memorials 1904, vol. I, 220-11
6. DGR Letters, 61.17
7. DGR Letters, 61.48
8. Howitt 1889, vol. II, 143; Boyce 2019, vol. II, 1057
9. EES to DGR, 1861, Troxell Collection of Rossetti MS, (29/19), Princeton University Library
10. EBJ Memorials 1904, vol. I, 231
11. DGR Letters, 62.03
12. Quoted WMR 1906, vol. I, 194-5
13. All details from the inquest
14. William Rossetti to F. G. Stephens, 15 February 1862, *Selected Letters of William Michael Rossetti*, ed. R. W. Peattie, 1990, #76
15. EBJ Memorials 1904, vol. I, 237
16. Shonfield 1987, 112

CHAPTER 10

1. DGR Letters, 68

WORKS CITED

Angeli 1949: Helen Rossetti Angeli, *Dante Gabriel Rossetti: His Friends and Enemies*, 1949

Atlay 1903: *Sir Henry Wentworth Acland A Memoir*, ed. J. B. Atlay, 1903

Battersby 2022: G. E. Battersby, 'Rossetti and Siddal: Reconsidering the Rift 1858–1860', *Journal of Pre-Raphaelite Studies* (31), Fall 2022

Baum 1932:an analytical list of MSS in Duke University Library, 1931

Bennett 1861: *James Henry Bennett, Mentone and the Riviera as a winter climate*, 1861

Boyce 2019: *The Boyce Papers: the Letters and Diaries of Joanna Boyce, Henry Wells and George P. Boyce*, ed. Sue Bradbury, 2 vols., 2019

Cook and Wedderburn 1909: *Collected Works of John Ruskin, Letters I and II*, ed. A. J. Cook and A. O. Wedderburn, 1909

DGR Letters: *Correspondence of Dante Gabriel Rossetti*, ed. W. E. Fredeman et al. ,10 vols., 2002–15. Citations by year and letter no.

EBJ Memorials 1904: *Memorials of Edward Burne-Jones*, ed. G. Burne-Jones, 2 vols, 1904

Edwards 1977: Marion Edwards, 'Elizabeth Siddal: the Age Problem', *Burlington Magazine*, February 1977

Edwards 1979: Marion Edwards, 'Elizabeth Siddal', *Family History*, April 1979

FMB Diary 1981: *The Diary of Ford Madox Brown*, ed. V. Surtees, 1981

Grylls 1964: Rosalie Glynn Grylls, *Portrait of Rossetti*, 1964

Hill 1897: *Letters of Dante Gabriel Rossetti to William Allingham*, ed. G. B. Hill, 1897

Holman-Hunt 1969: Diana Holman-Hunt, *My Grandfather, His Wives and Loves*, 1969

Howitt 1889: *Mary Howitt: An Autobiography*, 1889

Hunt 1932: Violet Hunt: *Wife of Rossetti*, 1932

Ibbitt 1862: William Ibbitt, 'Death of Mrs D. G. Rossetta [sic]', *Sheffield and Rotherham Independent*, 18 February 1862, reprinted *Sheffield Telegraph* 28 February 1862

JGM 1899: *Life and Letters of Sir John Everett Millais*, ed. J. G. Millais, 2 vols., 1899

Knight 1887: Joseph Knight, *The Life of Dante Gabriel Rossetti*, 1887

Lee 1955: Amice Lee, *Laurels and Rosemary: The Life of William and Mary Howitt*, 1955

Marillier 1904: revised edn of H. C. Marillier, *Dante Gabriel Rossetti: illustrated Memorial of his Life and Work*, 1899

Marsh 1986: Jan Marsh, *Pre-Raphaelite Sisterhood*, 1986 and 2010

Marsh 1989: Jan Marsh, *The Legend of Elizabeth Siddal*, 1989 and 2010

Marsh 1991: Jan Marsh, *Elizabeth Siddal Pre-Raphaelite Artist 1829–1862*, 1991

Marsh 1995: Jan Marsh, 'Art, Ambition, Sisterhood', *Women in the Victorian Art World*, ed. C. Campbell Orr, 1995

Marsh 2019: Jan Marsh, *Pre-Raphaelite Sisters*, ed. J. Marsh, 2019

Miller 1877: William Miller, *Wintering in the Riviera, with Notes of Travel in Italy and France, and Practical Hints to Travellers*, 1877

Norton 1913: *The Letters of Charles Eliot Norton*, ed. S. Norton et al, 2 vols., 1913

Shonfield 1987: Zuzanna Shonfield, *The Precariously Privileged: A Professional Family in Victorian London*, 1987

Trowbridge 2018: *My Ladys Soul: the Poems of Elizabeth Eleanor Siddall* (sic), ed. Serena Trowbridge, 2018

WA 1907: *William Allingham, A Diary*, eds. H. Allingham and D. Radford, 1907

Scott 1892: *Autobiographical Notes of the Life of William Bell Scott 1830-1882*, ed. W. Minto, 2 vols., 1892

WHH 1886: William Holman Hunt, 'Pre-Raphaelitism: A Fight for Art', *Contemporary Review*, April–June 1886

WHH 1905: William Holman Hunt, *Pre-Raphaelitism and the Pre-Raphaelite Brotherhood*, 2 vols., 1905 and revised 1913

WMR 1895, *Dante Gabriel Rossetti: his Family Letters with a Memoir*, ed. William M. Rossetti, 2 vols., 1895

WMR 1899: *Rossetti, Ruskin, Pre-Raphaelitism: Papers 1854-1862*, ed. William M. Rossetti, 1899

WMR 1901: *The Germ. A reprint*, ed. William M. Rossetti

WMR 1903 (1): *Rossetti Papers*, ed. William M. Rossetti

WMR 1903 (2): William M. Rossetti, 'Dante Rossetti and Elizabeth Siddal', *Burlington Magazine*, June 1903

WMR 1906: William M. Rossetti, *Some Reminiscences*, 2 vols., 1906

LIST OF ILLUSTRATIONS

brown ink with brown wash on paper, 170 x 195 mm, National Gallery of Canada, Ottawa

p. 31 See p. 1

p. 33 D. G. Rossetti, *Caricature of Himself Posing at Chatham Place for Siddal to Draw His Portrait*, 1853, ink on paper, 109 x 175 mm, Birmingham Museum and Art Gallery

p. 34 E. E. Siddal, *Pippa Passes*, 1854, pen and brown ink on off-white paper, 234 x 298 mm, Ashmolean Museum, Oxford

p. 37 E. E. Siddal, *Study for Clerk Saunders*, 1854, materials, dimensions and location unknown, reproduced from glass plate negative at Ashmolean Museum, Oxford

p. 38 D. G. Rossetti, *Figure Study of Elizabeth Siddal sitting*, 1854, graphite and ink on paper, 234 x 180 mm, Fitzwilliam Museum, Cambridge

p. 39 D. G. Rossetti, *Figure Study of Elizabeth Siddal reading*, 1854, graphite and ink on paper, 242 x 290 mm, Fitzwilliam Museum, Cambridge

p. 40 (left) A. M. Howitt, *Study of Elizabeth Siddal*, 1854, pencil on paper, 130 x 120 mm, Mark Samuels Lasner Collection, University of Delaware, Newark, DE

p. 40 (centre) B. L. Smith Bodichon, *Study of Elizabeth Siddal*, 1854, pencil on paper, 120 x 90 cm, Mark Samuels Lasner Collection, University of Delaware, Newark, DE

p. 40 (right) D. G. Rossetti, *Study of Elizabeth Siddal*, 1854, pencil on paper, 120 x 90 cm, Mark Samuels Lasner Collection, University of Delaware, Newark, DE

p. 41 E. E. Siddal, *Lovers Listening to Music*, 1854, pencil, pen and ink on paper, 378 x 398 mm, National Trust, Wightwick Manor, Wolverhampton

p. 42 E. E. Siddal, *Study for Sister Helen*, date unknown, materials, dimensions and location unknown, reproduced from glass plate negative at Ashmolean Museum, Oxford

p. 44 E. E. Siddal, *Madonna and Christ Child*, *c.* 1855, watercolour and pencil on paper, 64 x 57 mm, courtesy Maas Gallery, London

p. 45 E. E. Siddal, *Madonna and Christ Child*, *c.* 1855, watercolour on paper, 179 x 97 mm, Ashmolean Museum, Oxford

p. 46 D. G. Rossetti, *Study of Elizabeth Siddal Asleep in a Chair*, *c.* 1850-60, ink on paper, 170 x 109 cm, Birmingham Museum and Art Gallery

p. 47 See p. 9

p. 48 D. G. Rossetti, *Girl Singing to a Lute*, 1853, watercolor, gouache and gum arabic on paper, 220 x 100 mm, private collection

p. 49 (left) D. G. Rossetti, *Dante's Vision of Rachel and Leah*, 1855, watercolour on paper, 352 x 314 mm, Tate, London

p. 49 (right) D. G. Rossetti, *Passover in the Holy Family* (unfinished), 1855-6, watercolour on paper, 406 x 432 mm, Tate, London

p. 50 D. G. Rossetti, *Portrait of His Mother, Frances Rossetti*, 1853, pen and ink on paper, 127 x 102 mm, Birmingham Museum and Art Gallery

p. 51 J. E. Millais, *Portrait of John Ruskin* (detail), 1853-4, oil on canvas, 71.3 x 60.8 cm, Ashmolean Museum, Oxford

p. 53 Cover of the second edition of *Poem's by Alfred Tennyson*, commonly known as 'Moxon's Tennyson', 1859

p. 54 E. E. Siddal, *Study for Jephtha's Daughter*, *c.* 1855, graphite on paper, 212 x 119 mm, Delaware Art Museum, Wilmington, DE

p. 53 Anon., vintage postcard showing Clevedon pier and beach, *c.* 1905, private collection

p. 56 D. G. Rossetti, *The Annunciation*, 1855, watercolour, pencil, gum arabic and bodycolour on paper, 356 x 248 mm, Agnew's, London

p. 57 D. G. Rossetti, *Elizabeth Siddal*, 6 February 1855, pen and ink on paper, 130 x 112 mm, Ashmolean Museum, Oxford

p. 59 D. G. Rossetti, *Self-Portrait*, 20 September 1855, ink on paper, 129 x 115 mm, Fitzwilliam Museum, Cambridge

p. 60 A.-A.-E. Disdéri, *View of Fine Art Section, Exposition Universelle, Paris*, 1855, photograph, Bibliothèque Nationale de France, Paris

p. 62 D. G. Rossetti, *Paolo and Francesca da Rimini* (detail), 1855, watercolour on paper, 254 x 449 mm, Tate, London

p. 63 E. E. Siddal, *Sketch for Descent from the Cross*, *c.* 1855, pen and black ink and brown wash on paper, 197 x 140 mm, private collection

p. 66 Jean Gilletta, *General View of Town and Port of Menton*, *c.* 1900, photograph, Bibliothèque nationale de France, Paris

p. 68 D. G. Rossetti, *Arthur's Tomb*, also known as *Last Meeting of Lancelot and Guinevere*, 1855, watercolour on paper, 229 x 368 mm, British Museum, London

p. 69 D. G. Rossetti, *Illustration to Maids of Elfen-Mere*, 1854, graphite with pen and black ink and pen and brown ink on paper, 130 x 83 mm, Yale Collection of British Art, New Haven, CT

p. 71 E. E. Siddal, *Sir Patrick Spens*, 1856, watercolour on paper, 241 x 229 mm, Tate, London

p. 72 E. E. Siddal, *The Annuciation*, also known as *The Haunted Wood*, 1856, gouache on paper, 120 x 110 mm, National Trust, Wightwick Manor, Wolverhampton

p. 73 E. E. Siddal, *Lady Clare*, 1857, watercolour on paper, 338 x 254 mm, private collection

p. 74 E. E. Siddal, *St Agnes' Eve*, 1854, gouache on paper, 165 x 120 mm, National Trust, Wightwick Manor, Wolverhampton

p. 75 (left) E. E. Siddal, *Study for St Cecilia*, 1860, pen and ink on paper, 215 x 200 mm, National Trust, Wightwick Manor, Wolverhampton

p. 75 (right) D. G. Rossetti, *Study for St Cecilia*, 1856–7, pen and brown ink, 99 x 82 mm, Birmingham Museum and Art Gallery

p. 76 E. E. Siddal, compositional sketches, 1855, all in Ashmolean Museum, Oxford. Left: *Figures in Lightweight Skiffs*, pen and black ink on paper, 116 x 183 mm. Right: Two studies for the *Ruined Chapel*, illustrating Tennyson's poem 'Sir Galahad', approximately 180 x 130 mm and 180 x 155 mm

p. 77 E. E. Siddal and D. G. Rossetti, *Sir Galahad*, *c.* 1855, watercolour, 280 x 238 mm, private collection

p. 82 D. G. Rossetti, *Hamlet and Ophelia*, 1857–8, illustration to Shakespeare's *Hamlet*, pen and black ink on paper, 309 x 261 mm, British Museum, London

p. 83 E. E. Siddal, *Clerk Saunders*,

1857, watercolour, bodycolour and coloured chalks on paper, 284 x 181 mm, Fitzwilliam Museum, Cambridge

p. 88 D. G. Rossetti, *Study for the Quest of the Holy Grail*, 1857, pen and brown ink with graphite on paper, 250 x 351 mm, British Museum, London

p. 89 D. G. Rossetti, *Study for the Angel Holding the Holy Grail*, 1857, pen and ink with graphite on paper, 227 x 136 mm, Fitzwilliam Museum, Cambridge

p. 90 *Queen Street Chapel, as improved 1853*, 1853, lithograph by Parkin and Bacon

p. 91 William Ibbitt (after), *South East View of Sheffield, 1855*, 1885, lithograph, dimensions unknown

p. 92 *Sheffield School of Art,* lithograph, published *Illustrated Times,* 22 November 1856

p. 92 Anon., *Young Mitchell*, *c.* 1860, photograph, measurements unknown, Sheffield City Archives

p 93 (left) Anon., *Painting Studio*, *c.* 1905, photograph, measurements unknown, Sheffield City Archives

p 93 (right) Anon., *Painting Studio*, *c.* 1917, photograph, measurements unknown, Sheffield City Archives

p. 94 E. E. Siddal, *The Macbeths*, 1858–60?, pen and brush, Indian ink with scratching out, 214 x 135 mm, Ashmolean Museum, Oxford

p. 95 D. G. Rossetti, *Study for Sir Launcelot in the Queen's Chamber, (portrait of Jane Burden, later Morris)*, 1857, pencil with touches of ink on paper, 483 x 400 mm, Manchester City Art Gallery

p. 96 *Mr Cartledge's Lime Tree View*, 1863 advertisement, measurements unknown, courtesy Ann Andrews

p. 97 (left) E. E. Siddal, *Virgin and Child with Angel*, *c.* 1856, watercolour, gouache and metallic paint on paper, 197 x 152 mm, Delaware Art Museum, Wilmington, DE

p. 97 (right) D. G. Rossetti, *A Christmas Carol*, 1857, watercolour and gouache on paper, 343 x 297 mm, Harvard Art Museums/Fogg Museum, Cambridge, MA

p. 99 (left) E. E. Siddal, *Knight and Lady*, *c.* 1856, 137 x 137 mm, Tate, London

p. 99 (right) D. G. Rossetti, *Before the Battle*, 1858, watercolour on paper, 422 x 273 mm, Museum of Fine Arts, Boston, MA

p. 103 D. G. Rossetti, *Bocca Baciata (The Kissed Mouth)*, oil on panel, 32.1 x 27 cm, Museum of Fine Arts, Boston, MA

p. 109 Leicester's Hospital, Warwick, *c.* 1885, wood engraving, Wellcome Collection, London

p. 110 D. G. Rossetti, *How They Met Themselves*, 1860, pen and ink and wash on paper, 270 x 213 mm, Fitzwilliam Museum, Cambridge (Bridgeman)

p. 113 D. G. Rossetti, *Dr Johnson at the Mitre*, 1860, pen and black ink on paper, 222 x 217 mm, Fitzwilliam Museum, Cambridge

p. 114 (top) E. E. Siddal, *Study for Woeful Victory*, c. 1860, pen and pencil on paper, 164 x 126 mm, Cecil Higgins Art Gallery, Bedford, as reproduced in Marillier 1904

p. 114 (bottom) E. E. Siddal, *Study for Sister Helen*, date unknown, ink and chalk on paper, 150 x 130 mm, National Trust, Wightwick Manor, Wolverhampton

p. 115 G. Burne-Jones, *The Bridge of Sighs (Found Drowned)*, pencil, pen and black ink on paper, 143 x 178 mm, private collection

p. 118 D. G. Rossetti, *St George and Sabra*, 1857–60, watercolour on paper, 365 x 365 mm, Tate, London

p. 119 E. E. Siddal, *The Woeful Victory*, 1860, ink on paper, dimensions unknown, Mark Samuels Lasner Collection, Special Collections, University of Delaware, Newark, DE

p. 121 E. E. Siddal, *Study for The Blessed Damozel*, 1855, pencil on paper, 208 x 107 mm, Ashmolean Museum, Oxford

p. 125 D. G. Rossetti, *Algernon Swinburne*, 1861, watercolour on paper, 182 x 158 mm, Fitzwilliam Museum, Cambridge

p. 127 E. E. Siddal, *Figure of Rachel*, 1860, stud wall, lime plaster and paint layer in an organic medium, 180 x 400 cm, National Trust, Red House, Bexleyheath

p. 129 D. G. Rossetti, sketch of projected wallpaper design, 1860, as reproduced in DGR Letters, 61.05

p. 130 D. G. Rossetti, title-page design for his translations of Italian poems, *c.* 1861, pen and brown ink on paper, 147 x 89 mm, Museum of Fine Arts, Boston, MA

p. 131 E. E. Siddal, decorations to casket, *c.* 1859, paint on wood bound with studded iron bands, 17.7 x 29.2 x 17.7 cm, Kelmscott Manor, Oxfordshire

p. 136 D. G. Rossetti, *St George and Princess Sabra*, 1862, watercolour on paper, 524 x 308 mm, Tate, London

p. 137 D. G. Rossetti, *The First Madness of Ophelia*, also known as *Horatio Discovering the Madness of Ophelia*, 1864, watercolour and gum arabic on paper, 39.4 x 29.2 cm, Gallery Oldham

p. 141 Anon., *Rossetti family grave*, Highgate Cemetery, London, photograph courtesy Simon Edwards

p. 142 D. G. Rossetti, *Beata Beatrix*, 1872, oil on canvas, 87.5 x 69.3 cm, predella: 26.5 x 69.2 cm, Art Institute of Chicago, IL

p. 145 J. E. Millais, *Study for the Head of Ophelia*, 1852, pencil on paper, 232 x 307 mm, Birmingham Museum and Art Gallery

Unless otherwise noted, all images courtesy of the holding institution or collector, and/or Wikimedia

INDEX

Entries in *italic* denote illustrations

First published 2023 by
Pallas Athene (Publishers) Limited,
2 Birch Close,
London N19 5XD

www.pallasathene.co.uk

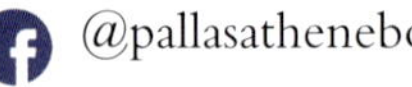 @pallasathenebooks 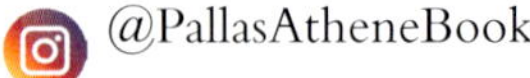 @PallasAtheneBooks

 @Pallas_books 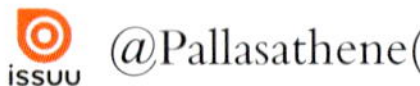 @Pallasathene()

Cover: Detail from D. G. Rossetti, *Sketch of Elizabeth Siddal at the Easel*, c. 1852, Nationalmuseum, Stockholm

ISBN 978 1 84368 231 8

Printed in England by Short Run Press